ALSO BY ALEX BEAM

American Crucifixion
Gracefully Insane
A Great Idea at the Time
The Russians Are Coming!
Fellow Travelers

The Feud

The Feud

Vladimir Nabokov, Edmund Wilson, and the End of a Beautiful Friendship

ALEX BEAM

PANTHEON BOOKS   NEW YORK

All rights reserved. Published in the United States by
Pantheon Books, a division of Penguin Random House LLC, New York,
and distributed in Canada by Random House of Canada,
a division of Penguin Random House Canada Limited, Toronto.

Pantheon Books and colophon are registered trademarks
of Penguin Random House LLC.

Grateful acknowledgment is made to The Overlook Press for permission
to reprint excerpts from *Eugene Onegin* by Alexander Pushkin,
translated by Walter Arndt. Translation copyright © 1972 by
Walter Arndt. Originally published in 1992 by The Overlook Press,
New York, NY (www.overlookpress.com). Reprinted by permission
of The Overlook Press. All rights reserved.

Library of Congress Cataloging-in-Publication Data
Name: Beam, Alex, author.
Title: The feud : Vladimir Nabokov, Edmund Wilson,
and the end of a beautiful friendship / Alex Beam.
Description: New York : Pantheon, 2016.
Includes bibliographical references and index.
Identifiers: LCCN 2016019850 (print). LCCN 2016007056 (ebook).
ISBN 9781101870228 (hardback) ISBN 9781101870235 (ebook).
Subjects: LCSH: Nabokov, Vladimir Vladimirovich, 1899–1977—
Friends and associates. Nabokov, Vladimir Vladimirovich, 1899–1977—
Criticism and interpretation. Wilson, Edmund, 1895–1972—
Friends and associates. Wilson, Edmund, 1895–1972—
Criticism and interpretation.
BISAC: BIOGRAPHY & AUTOBIOGRAPHY / Literary. HISTORY / Europe /
Russia & the Former Soviet Union. HISTORY / Modern / 20th Century.
Classification: LCC PS3527.A15 (print). LCC PS3527.A15 Z615 2016
(ebook). DDC 818/.5209—dc23.
LC record available at: lccn.loc.gov/2016019850.

www.pantheonbooks.com

Jacket illustration: Vladimir Nabokov: Gamma-Keystone/Getty Images;
Edmund Wilson: Granger, New York City
Jacket design by Kelly Blair

Printed in the United States of America
First Edition
2 4 6 8 9 7 5 3 1

To my friend, Michael V. Carlisle

Life has no pleasure higher or nobler than that of friendship. It is painful to consider, that this sublime enjoyment may be impaired or destroyed by innumerable causes, and that there is no human possession of which the duration is less certain.

—SAMUEL JOHNSON, "The Uncertainty of Friendship," 1758

Contents

Introduction

I first learned of the friendship and subsequent feud between Edmund Wilson and Vladimir Nabokov only a few years ago. A friend of mine had been tracking down Alexander Pushkin's descendants—there are a few—and mentioned in passing that Wilson and Nabokov had ended a quarter-century-long friendship because of a disagreement over how to translate Pushkin's novel in verse *Eugene Onegin*. I burst out laughing. It was the silliest thing I had ever heard.

I hadn't known about this famous contretemps because I was eleven years old in 1965, when Wilson trained his guns against his longtime comrade in letters—"a personal friend of Mr. Nabokov . . . an admirer of much of his work," as he introduced himself in a salvo of ill-will splattered across the pages of *The New York Review of Books*. I wasn't reading the *Review*, then in its third year of publication, and it certainly wasn't lying around my parents' house. I was reading *Boys' Life*, what the Russians would call the "organ" of the Boy Scouts of America. I think Vladimir Nabokov, he of the wondrous outdoorsy boyhood, would have approved.

I know a thing or two about Russian language and literature— my harshest readers will confirm that modest count—but I had never read *Onegin*, and was familiar with only the highest peaks of Nabokov's astonishing range: *Lolita* and *Speak, Memory*. There was a time when college students with literary pretensions read Edmund Wilson, but it wasn't my time. When I graduated in 1975, Wilson had been dead for three years, with his literary renown and influence already in deep eclipse.

Several years into this project, I laugh less now. Of course the pedantic exchanges between two eminent men of letters still ring silly—is *pochuya*, which could mean "sensing," or "sniffing," a present or past gerund? (Good question!) Did Pushkin know English well enough to read Byron? (Maybe.) But the end of a friendship is always a loss. Especially a friendship so deeply and mutually celebratory as this one. "Edmund was always in a state of joy when Vladimir appeared," Wilson's third wife, Mary McCarthy, recalled. "They had an absolute ball together. He loved him."[1] Their correspondence was legendary, full of rambunctious exchanges about literature, gossip, sex in taxicabs, sore gums, and very genuine emotions. "You are one of the few people in the world whom I keenly miss when I do not see them," Nabokov wrote to Wilson eight years into their friendship.[2]

And then, nothing.

Like so many intimate relationships, this one bore the seeds of its own destruction. In one of his very first letters to his new acquaintance, Wilson scores Nabokov for his punning, which Wilson finds tiresome. But of course it is irrepressible, and will continue throughout his life. Nabokov's last major novel, *Ada*—the title itself a pun, alluding to "ardor," and to the Russian *ah, da* (oh, yes)—mentions Mr. Eliot's famous poem, "The Waistline"; and so on, *ada infinitum*. In many ways the two men proved to be two entirely different and contradictory people, Wilson the erudite literalist and Nabokov the ludist, the fantasist, the trickster king. The opposites attracted, and then they didn't.

When their friendship ended, much was made of the fact that Wilson never reviewed any of Nabokov's novels. Indeed Nabokov himself complained in a gift inscription to Wilson, "Why do you never review my works?" But it is very hard to imagine Wilson enjoying, say, *The Gift*, Nabokov's favorite of his own Russian novels. *The Gift* would have infuriated Wilson. It is simultaneously a work of literary criticism, a memoir of the Russian emigration in Germany, and a complicated gloss on Pushkin's *Onegin*. *The Gift* incorporates a novella-length, jocoserious "biography" of Nikolai Chernyshevsky, a sacred figure of nineteenth-century socialism whom Nabokov mercilessly lampoons.

It is supremely Nabokovian; a novel, and not a novel. And it ends with a perfectly crafted *Onegin* stanza, Nabokov's knowing nod to his favorite Russian writer. That stanza appears on—but I anticipate.

It is equally hard to imagine Nabokov reading, savoring, or even understanding *Patriotic Gore*, Wilson's unsentimental, revisionist overview of the literature and the mythopoeia that animated the combatants in America's Civil War. Wilson spent more than ten years researching the book. It is difficult to envision Nabokov spending even ten minutes perusing its index. When *Gore* appeared in 1962, Nabokov had already ensconced himself in Switzerland, settled atop a pile of money from the fabulous sales of his novel *Lolita*. America, and Edmund Wilson, were only faintly visible in his rearview mirror.

LET ME MAKE two quick points:

Told from such a distance in time, this becomes a story of unequal combat. Nabokov is very much alive in his work, perhaps less on the night table than on the college syllabus, but nonetheless he remains known to millions. Not so Wilson. In the years leading up to his death in 1972, "he was not much read," his friend Jason Epstein wrote in a heartfelt obituary. Once hailed as the "dean of American letters," possessed of what the biographer Leon Edel called "a certain Johnsonian celebrity," Wilson is largely unknown today. When I mentioned Wilson's name to a participant at a donors' event at the Boston Public Library, his reply was: "It's weird how he makes everything about ants." No, that is Edward O. Wilson, the Harvard professor and author of *The Ants, The Anthill,* and *Journey to the Ants.* Edmund Wilson was someone else entirely.

Second: There seems to be an infectious tendency to "go Nabokovian" when writing about the late, great novelist. Andrew Field, Nabokov's first biographer, decided not to include an index with his biography, a complicated and annoying homage to his subject, who sometimes bent indexes to his own playful needs. When Wilson's biographer Jeffrey Meyers wrote about the Nabokov-Wilson feud, he couldn't resist the easily available pun "when Pushkin came to shovekin."[3] Douglas Hofstadter, the Pulitzer Prize–winning author of *Gödel, Escher, Bach,* who spent two years translating *Onegin* with great élan, fell into pun-ditry himself, asserting his right to "poetic lie-sense," and so on.

I myself succumbed. It is futile to resist the lure of such pseudo-verbs as "pedanitifies," or to ignore the temptation to tack footnote after footnote onto my explanation of *Onegin*'s scintillating "Pedal Digression." When I needed to cite an *Onegin* translation, I quoted from the late Walter Arndt's version, just because I knew that would irk the Nabokovian shade. Nabokov hated Arndt's *Onegin.* I call Vera Nabokov "Vera Nabokova" in part because that is how she signed her name, but also to fingernail-scratch the Elysian blackboard where the Master may currently be lecturing.

He inveighed against the feminization of Russian family names, and insisted on teaching *Anna Karenin*, never *Anna Karenina*.

These are pure Nabokovian impulses. Literary confrontations were to be pursued in this life and the next. When revising his *Onegin* translation after Wilson's death, Nabokov urged his publisher to shake a leg: "I would like to see my edition printed before confronting an irate Pushkin and a grinning E. Wilson beyond the cypress curtain."

A feud unto death, and beyond. As we shall see, Wilson attacked Nabokov from beyond the grave, affording himself a satisfaction we cannot yet fully appreciate. In the five years that he outlived Wilson, Nabokov, too, tap-danced on his old rival's tombstone, in a manner unbecoming the international celebrity and self-proclaimed genius that he was. And then Nabokov's son, Dmitri—but again, I anticipate.

In a famous essay, Ralph Waldo Emerson wrote that "friendship, like the immortality of the soul, is too good to be believed."

In the case of Nabokov and Wilson, it was.

The Feud

1

The Beginning

This is how it began. It is worth recording because Vladimir Nabokov would later offer up an alternate version of how he came to be friends with Edmund Wilson.

Wilson knew Nicolas Nabokov ("emotionally extravagant, physically demonstrative, and always late"),[1] an émigré composer who achieved some renown in the United States and Europe after fleeing Russia. In 1939 Nabokov rented a house across the street from Wilson in the Cape Cod town of Wellfleet, Massachusetts, and they inevitably met. Nabokov had written music for the Ballets Russes and the New York Philharmonic. Their shared acquaintances included the Oxford don Isaiah Berlin and W. H. Auden, who had recently moved to the United States.

Wilson would have bearded the charismatic, extroverted composer because he was fascinated by Russia. As with many American intellectuals, the Soviet Union's "new society," being built atop the ruins of czarist Russia, entranced him. The Great Depression had laid America low, and Wilson had seen its depredations firsthand. He had visited Russia for a few months in 1935, and had time to study the language while recovering from scarlet fever in an Odessa hospital for six weeks.

Wilson liked Russian language and literature, and he liked Russians, too. So it was the most natural thing in the world that Nicolas Nabokov would reach out to Wilson on behalf of a relative, in a famous August 1940 note.

Nicolas reported that his cousin Vladimir had recently arrived in the United States, and was in dire financial straits. "I await a miracle or I will lose all hope," Nicolas wrote, quoting Vladimir. "Help," Nicolas wrote twice, in Russian. "Help, dear Edmund Edmundovich. Do whatever you can."

Wilson did help. When Vladimir wrote to him from a Russian friend's summer house in Vermont, Wilson proposed a fall meeting in New York. The two men met in early October, and before the year was out, Wilson, filling in as literary editor of *The New Republic*, had commissioned a review from Vladimir. Wilson was quickly smitten. "I'm amazed at the excellence of the book reviews he's been doing for me," he wrote to his Princeton literature professor and mentor, Christian Gauss. "He is a brilliant fellow."[2] Soon the two men started talking about a joint translation of Alexander Pushkin's famous "little tragedy," *Mozart and Salieri*, which the magazine published in 1941. "It is quite perfect now," Nabokov wrote to Wilson when he saw the finished product. "You have played your Mozart to my Salieri."

Wilson boosted more than one Nabokov. He also promoted Nicolas's career, publishing his music criticism in *The New Republic*, and helping him place reviews in *The Atlantic Monthly*. Wilson tried to convince his friend Thornton Wilder to write a libretto for Nicolas, based on Alexander Pushkin's unfinished novel, *The Blackamoor of Peter the Great*. When Wilder demurred, Wilson briefly considered taking on the job himself.[3]

Just six months after their first meeting, Vladimir Nabokov and Wilson were chaffing each other like old pals. Wilson praised

Nabokov's first submissions, but warned him to "refrain from puns, to which I see you have a slight propensity. They are pretty much excluded from serious journalism here." Wilson had just published *To the Finland Station*, his classic sympathetic overview of the origins of European and Russian Marxism. He sent his new friend an inscribed copy: "To Vladimir Nabokov, in the hope that this may make him think better of Lenin."[4] Nabokov replied that he had enjoyed parts of the book, but could not stomach Wilson's treacly depiction of Vladimir Ilyich Lenin ("He knew how to talk to the country people . . . good at chess but did not care about winning") to pass unnoticed. "Now we come to Ilyitch—and here I itch (sorry)," Nabokov wrote. "Not even the magic of your style has made me like him." For Nabokov "Leninist reality," as the Soviets liked to call it, would always be "a pail of milk of human kindness with a dead rat at the bottom."

A few months later Nicolas Nabokov wrote again to Wilson: "I can't tell you how endlessly grateful I am for what you have done for the 'new' Nabokov. He wrote me an enthusiastic letter about you." Nicolas addressed his correspondent as "mon cher Huileson," a play on the French word for "oil," and signed his name "Nab O' Cough." Punning ran in the family.

WHO WAS EDMUND WILSON in 1940? Although history would later reverse their order of importance, he was older—forty-five years old to Nabokov's forty—more famous, and arguably more accomplished than Vladimir Nabokov at that time. Coincidentally both men's fathers were prominent jurists. Wilson's father, a pathologically neurotic lawyer, served as New Jersey's attorney general under Woodrow Wilson, who supposedly promised to elevate him to the U.S. Supreme Court during his presidency.[5]

(Nabokov's grandfather was Russia's minister of justice under the reformist czar Alexander II, and his father, an expert on the Russian criminal code, served briefly as minister of justice in the breakaway Crimean Republic after the Russian Revolution.) Wilson's mother, née Helen Kimball, never really warmed to her only child, with whom she often squabbled about money. She had money. Wilson wanted her to share it with him. She declined. "A woman of limited intelligence, prosaic, self-confident and self-assured," according to Wilson's friend and literary executor Leon Edel, "she never read Edmund's writings."[6] She saddled her russet-haired young child with the nickname "Bunny," which she liked to repeat in front of his friends. Wilson never much cared for the name. On the final day of her life, Helen Wilson warned her granddaughter Rosalind not to marry a writer "because you'll never have any money."[7]

Wilson had breezed through the Hill School in Pennsylvania and Princeton University, emerging as a remarkably well-educated man. He knew Latin and Greek well and French superbly, and started publishing literary criticism shortly after graduation. His first book, an appreciation of Wallace Stevens and e. e. cummings, appeared when he was twenty-six. At twenty-nine he wrote in his diary: "On the train [to California] I read Sophocles' *Electra* in Greek."[8]

Like Ernest Hemingway and John Dos Passos, he served in the ambulance service during World War I, then returned to New York to launch his career as a journalist and literary critic. He was a gifted talent spotter for a golden age of American letters, promoting the careers of Hemingway, his Princeton classmate F. Scott Fitzgerald, and the poet Edna St. Vincent Millay, with whom he pursued a tempestuous, on-again off-again love affair. Wilson was among the first American critics to champion the

The thirty-seven-year-old Edmund Wilson with members of the Delegation for Independent Miners' Relief Committee, 1932. Wilson is sitting at the left, Malcolm Cowley on the right. *(Beinecke Library, Yale University)*

"difficult" James Joyce, in his famous overview of modern literature, *Axel's Castle*, published in 1931.

If we remember him today, we probably recall Wilson as the ruddy-faced jowly critic staring disapprovingly from the inside back flyleaf of an assigned library text. But in his twenties and thirties he was a certified member of Manhattan's smart set. He worked first for Frank Crowninshield's legendary *Vanity Fair*, then moved over to the more progressive *New Republic*. He was a mandarin but not a snob, writing with equal enthusiasm about *Finnegans Wake*, which he liked, and Agatha Christie's detective stories, which he found tiresome. Wilson, who could discuss "Dante and Catullus and Verlaine without standing on tiptoe," Norman Podhoretz wrote, "is also the man who can without stooping produce an article on Farfariello, who was doing impersonations in Italian at the Fugazi Theater" on Manhattan's Lower East Side.[9]

The Great Depression left an indelible mark on Wilson, not because he suffered particularly, but because he traveled to parts of America where the damage was greatest. Wilson, along with fellow writers John Dos Passos, Malcolm Cowley, and Theodore Dreiser, visited Harlan County, Kentucky, to report on the 1931 coal strike and the miners' abject living conditions. These were writers *engagés;* in addition to packing his notebooks, Wilson brought food and clothing for the miners. (Dreiser brought a girlfriend, which resulted in an adultery charge.) Sheriffs' deputies chased Wilson out of Harlan, threatening him with jail time and worse.

The next year Wilson published his fourth book, *The American Jitters: A Year of the Slump,* comprising dispatches from San Diego, Brooklyn, West Virginia, and the brave new world of Detroit, where Henry Ford was brazenly reinventing capitalism in the teeth of the world crisis. "So far as I can see," Wilson wrote, "Karl Marx's predictions are coming true." In 1932 Wilson, Dos Passos, and Sherwood Anderson circulated their "Writers' Manifesto," calling for "a temporary dictatorship of the class-conscious workers. . . . We declare ourselves supporters of the social-economic revolution," they wrote, "such revolution being an immediate step toward the creation in the United States of a new human culture based on common material possession."

Jitters ended with a remarkable chapter, "The Case of the Author," in which Wilson applied "the Marxist formula" to himself, "as a specimen of the American bourgeoisie." He noted, for instance, that his father eschewed investments and speculations, "and one of the results of this has been that I have grown up in modern prosperous America with a slightly outside point of view." He explained that he enlisted in World War I "not because I cared much about the War, but because . . . I wanted to get away from my old life." He signed up as an enlisted man instead of attending officers' school because that was what "most of my friends from college were doing," and "I wanted to get as far away from that old life as possible. . . . I swore to myself that when the War was over I should stand outside society altogether. . . . I should devote myself to the great human interests which transcended standards of living and conventions: Literature, History. The Creation of Beauty, the Discovery of Truth."[10]

The young Wilson scolded himself for his bourgeois lifestyle. His work for "highbrow magazines" netted him about $7,500 a year (slightly over $100,000 today), but he allowed that family inheritances provided an extra "margin for classical reading, liquor, and general irresponsibility. And as I have got used to these bourgeois luxuries, I naturally shrink from the prospect of an era where everybody will have to earn all he gets." Said era was approaching, he predicted: "The money-making period of American history has definitely come to an end. Capitalism has run its course." The new proletarian thinkers "look to Russia," Wilson wrote, and so did he: "I, though I am a bourgeois myself . . . have certain interests in common with these proletarians. I, too, admire the Russian Communist leaders."

Inevitably the next stop would be Russia, as it was for so many of his peers. Although he never joined the American Communist Party, Wilson voted for its candidate, William Z. Foster, in the 1932 election. His sympathies lay on the left for most of his life. Funded by a two-thousand-dollar Guggenheim Foundation grant, Wilson sailed from London intending to study at the Institute for Marxism-Leninism in Moscow, which turned out to be closed to foreigners. Instead Wilson traveled around the country for several months, writing dispatches that were eventually collected in parts of two books, *Travels in Two Democracies* (1936) and *Red, Black, Blond and Olive; Studies in Four Civilizations: Zuni, Haiti, Soviet Russia, Israel* (1956). The dates are significant because Wilson, a self-described "visiting journalist known to be sympathetic with the Soviet regime," censored many passages in 1936 that showed up in print twenty years later.

With the cruelty of hindsight, we can say that Wilson got off on the wrong foot. In Moscow he stayed in the temporarily unoccupied apartment of Walter Duranty, the notorious *New York Times* correspondent who completely failed to grasp the horror of Stalin's tyranny. Ever the reporter, Wilson did notice the signed photograph of Stalin on Duranty's bookcase.

Wilson knew that he was witnessing a historic turning point in Soviet history, but like so many foreigners on the scene, he didn't understand what was really going on. His journalistic antennae correctly discerned that "the atmosphere of fear and suspicion . . . has evidently become more tense since the [Sergei] Kirov assassination"—the 1934 killing of one of Stalin's rivals, now assumed to have been engineered by Stalin. Wilson infelicitously concluded that the sense of paranoia was "of course . . . no worse than Hollywood (though the penalties—death and deportation—are greater). Stalin and [Lazar] Kaganovitch are hardly more sacred names in Moscow than Schulberg and Thalberg are on the Coast."[11]

Hollywood is a tough town. But no one got a bullet to the back of the head for botching a movie script.

Strolling through Moscow's Park of Culture and Rest, Wilson remarked to a Russian companion that the assembled holiday-makers seemed to be quite subdued. "She replied in a low voice,

'C'est que tout le monde a très peur' " ("It's because everyone is very frightened"). Wilson censored that remark in 1936 but published it in the 1956 collection.[12]

Wilson's observation that "you feel in the Soviet Union that you are living at the moral top of the world, where the light never really goes out" would haunt him for the rest of his life. Only later—much later—did he temper his enthusiasm for Things Soviet. He never fully surrendered his admiration for Lenin, for which Nabokov attacked him on first acquaintance. The first time Wilson saw Lenin's waxy effigy preserved in Red Square, he enthused: "The head in the tomb, with its high forehead, its straight nose, its pointed beard . . . its sensitive nostrils and eyelids, gives an impression in some ways similar to that one gets from the supposed death-mask of Shakespeare. It is a beautiful face, of exquisite fineness, and—what surely proves its authenticity—it is profoundly aristocratic."[13]

Wilson's Russia stay ended with him flat on his back for six weeks in an Odessa hospital. This was probably the only time that Wilson systematically studied the Russian language, surrounded as he was by non-English speakers. Many years later he recalled that "I learned Russian, primarily, I think, in order to read Pushkin," the Shakespeare of Russian letters.[14]

What else do we need to know about the forty-five-year-old Wilson? The boundless eclecticism—his detractors would call it high-minded dilettantism—had not yet taken over his career. In later middle age he would dive into Haitian literature, learn Hungarian and Hebrew,* the latter language to ease his way into two books about the Dead Sea Scrolls, and immerse himself in the his-

---

* The Hebrew inscription on Wilson's headstone in the Wellfleet cemetery reads, "Be strong, be strong, and may we be strengthened," a phrase traditionally repeated at the end of a Torah reading.

tory of upstate New York, where he lived in his mother's home for
about half the year, starting in the early 1950s. Wilson's enthusiasms extended to the supernatural. "He was very much interested
in the Abominable Snowman and wished that he were up to asking The New Yorker to send him on an assignment to track down
reports of this fascinating creature," according to his friend, the
Harvard American studies professor Daniel Aaron, who accompanied Wilson on a reporting trip to the Iroquois Nation. Well
before the famous protests at Wounded Knee, South Dakota, Wilson had become a fervid supporter of Native American rights. In
the final decade of his life he rededicated himself to denouncing
American capitalism and its infernal paymaster, the Internal Revenue Service.

That was in the future. In 1940 Wilson was a compact fire-
plug of seemingly boundless energy. He was quite the ladies' man,
already embroiled in his third marriage, this time to the fiery
young writer Mary McCarthy. He had previously married a beautiful actress, who seemed to be on tour for much of their marriage.
His second wife died in a freak accident. Wilson pursued innumerable extra- and intramarital affairs, which complicated his life
enormously. He chronicled his many conquests in his unprudish
diary, published posthumously "(*Marie:* I could feel her vagina
throbbing powerfully—Thrust naked cock up into those obscure
and meaty regions"[15]). He "thought constantly of sex,"[16] he confessed. Marriage was a commitment that Wilson didn't take very
seriously. Wilson's daughter Rosalind remembered his first wife,
the actress Mary Blair, coming "home from the theater to find a
DO NOT DISTURB sign on the door and that my father was still
seeing Edna Millay, with whom he was in love for many years."[17]
Wife number two, Margaret Canby, said of him: "You're a cold,
fishy leprous person, Bunny Wilson."[18]

Wilson viewed himself as both a creator and a critic, but the world thought otherwise. In 1929 he published his first novel, *I Thought of Daisy*, which he had been nurturing for years. Even his lover Millay, thinly disguised as the bohemian poet "Rita Cavanaugh," found the book to be uneven. It became clear, as Wilson's sympathetic biographer Lewis Dabney wrote, that "Wilson was never quite at ease with 'invented' characters."[19]

Wilson had a prickly disposition. "His candor may have exceeded his tact," his friend Aaron once wrote.[20] It was true. Addressing Fitzgerald on the subject of his new novel, *This Side of Paradise*, Wilson said, "Your hero as intellectual is a fake of the first water . . ."[21] His posthumously published diaries have an initially transgressive flavor. For instance, his descriptions of making love to his many wives and mistresses seem prurient, although on further consideration they feel honest in a way that the fictional sex scenes in his "bawdy" novel, *Memoirs of Hecate County*, never do. Still in his twenties, he wrote a letter to the grand grizzly of American letters, H. L. Mencken, correcting the famous dictionarist on his misuse of "jejune": "By the way, why do you always use 'jejune' as if it meant 'juvenile' or 'callow'? This has been worrying me for years."[22] In later life he noted that his fourth wife, Elena, called certain people "limited." Wilson called them stupid.

Reproach, and self-reproach, came easily to Wilson. But where his first love, literature, was concerned, he often exhibited a generosity of spirit. Yes, he could criticize Fitzgerald, but it was Wilson who edited his late friend's unfinished novel *The Last Tycoon*, to provide money for Fitzgerald's widow and daughter. He likewise assembled the book *The Crack-Up* from Fitzgerald's unpublished essays and letters, for the benefit of his friend's estate. A profligate spender who was almost always short of cash, Wilson nevertheless insisted that his five-thousand-dollar *Tycoon* fee be paid into Fitzgerald's royalty account, set up for Zelda and her daughter, Scottie.

It is true that Wilson seized on Nabokov, the brilliant apparition from another world, because Nabokov interested him, and not everyone did. But he also offered to help Nabokov because he recognized a kindred spirit in need, and because it was the right thing to do.

WHO WAS VLADIMIR NABOKOV in 1940? That is a more complicated question. Like Wilson, he enjoyed a superb education, not only at the Tenishev School in St. Petersburg, but also from his father, who, like the father in Nabokov's autobiographical novel *The Gift,* "knew Pushkin as some people know the liturgy." (Nabokov called his real father "a torrent of Pushkin iambics.") Nabokov and Pushkin seemed to have been conjoined at birth. Vladimir was born in 1899, during the heady centennial festivities for Russia's greatest poet. As a young boy he composed a "Don Juan's list" of his female conquests, in imitation of Pushkin, and so on.

Nabokov's father served in Russia's provisional government of 1917, following the quasi-democratic February revolution. In November the Bolsheviks seized power, arrested the elder Nabokov, and then released him. The family fled St. Petersburg, then Russia itself, when Lenin and the Bolsheviks seized power in a coup d'état. Like many aristocratic families, the Nabokovs drifted southward during Russia's brutal civil war, when it seemed possible that White Russian armies might succeed in rolling back Soviet power. After a few blissful months, which he spent butterfly collecting on the grounds of two different estates on the Crimean Peninsula, Vladimir and his family escaped Russia in

1919, in a steamer raked by Bolshevik machine-gun fire. Nabokov liked to recall that he and his father were playing chess on deck as the *Nadyezhda* (*Hope*) slid out of Sevastopol Harbor, and out of machine-gun range. Perhaps that was even true.

The Nabokovs initially fetched up in England, where Vladimir entered Trinity College, Cambridge, his education financed in part by the progressive sales of his mother's formidable cache of jewelry. While he and his brother Sergey studied in England, the family moved to Berlin, then teeming with an estimated four hundred thousand Russian émigrés.

Nabokov had mixed feelings about the émigrés with whom he shared the next twenty years of his life in Berlin, Prague, and Paris. He insisted that, unlike them, he didn't regret losing his family's fortune and heady social standing in the upheaval of 1917. His losses were, however, very real. When he was just seventeen years old, an uncle left him a two-thousand-acre estate, a manor house, and investments that would be worth more than $100 million today.[23] But Nabokov felt he had lost something far more precious: the connection to his fairy-tale childhood, so lovingly re-created in the memoir *Speak, Memory*. And he had lost the connection to his true mother tongue: "My private tragedy," he called it.[24]

Nabokov famously never had a home. In the United States he and his wife, Vera, always rented. At Cornell University in Ithaca, New York, where he taught for a decade, they occupied homes vacated by professors on sabbatical. The Nabokovs ended their days in a small suite of rooms at the Montreux Palace Hotel in Switzerland. When asked to explain his peripatetic life of exile, Nabokov said, "Nothing short of a replica of my childhood surroundings would have satisfied me." His hero Pushkin was a wanderer, too, exiled from St. Petersburg by the czar for years at a time. Like Nabokov, "To the end of his life he remained deeply attached to what he considered his real home, the Lyceum, and to his former fellow students."[25]

In a loss as tragic as that of his childhood, Nabokov's father was killed soon after he left Russia. Two right-wing monarchist gunmen burst into a political event in Berlin at which the older Vladimir Nabokov was speaking. The men intended to murder Pavel Milyukov, another exiled parliamentarian speaking at the rally, whom they held responsible for the overthrow of the czar. The elder Nabokov wrestled one of the assassins to the ground, but the second man shot him three times. Milyukov lived, Nabokov's father died. At the age of twenty-two Vladimir Nabokov found himself more or less alone in the world.*

He chose the most parlous profession of them all: writing. Supplementing his income by tutoring, translating, and even teaching tennis, Nabokov became one of the best-known novelists of the Russian emigration. Writing as "Vladimir Sirin," he published nine novels in twelve years, some of which later came to be regarded as masterpieces. Sirin was a success, seeing his work translated into five languages, including English. In 1941 the American publisher Bobbs-Merrill retitled the British translation of *Camera Obscura* for an American audience: *Laughter in the Dark*. It disappeared without a trace.[26]

Nabokov had written his own *Finland Station*, the notorious, discursive chapter 4 of *The Gift*, but neither Wilson nor anyone else had ever read it. Chapter 4 lampooned the career of Nikolai Chernyshevsky, regarded by many as the father of Russian

---

* Nabokov's wife, Vera, owned a small pistol that she often carried in her handbag. Their friend Jason Epstein thinks she intended to protect her husband from the fate that befell his father: "Why else would you sit at the back of every lecture with a gun in your purse? She was prepared to kill the assassin."

socialism. Émigré editors refused to publish the Chernyshevsky profile without significant changes. Nabokov adamantly refused. He thought Chernyshevsky was a loser and a phony. As for the nineteenth-century radical writers so beloved by Wilson, they "write with their feet," Nabokov said. Chapter 4 finally appeared in Russian in 1952, a decade and a half after it was written.

Nabokov created, prolifically, in conditions that would have daunted anyone else. He sometimes composed his fiction or poetry in longhand, sitting atop a toilet seat, while his wife and baby son slept a few feet away in their one-room Berlin apartment. Decades later, when the Wilson-Nabokov feud burned white-hot with loathing, Wilson observed that "the miseries, horrors and handicaps that [Nabokov] has had to confront in his exile would have degraded or broken many, but these have been overcome by his fortitude and his talent."*[27]

Nabokov's father was a devoted Anglophile, and, like his son, quite at home in the King's English. Nabokov *père* wrote a series of articles ("Charles Dickens: A Russian Appreciation") that appeared in the *Dickensian* magazine in 1912. Vladimir claimed that the first language he heard was English, read to him from children's books in early childhood. Father and young son both loved butterflies, and the boy hovered over copies of the London journal *The Entomologist* the way his peers (like my own father) might have cherished copies of *St. Nicholas*, the turn-of-the-century storybook magazine for children.

As he entered his thirties, still treading water financially, Vladimir saw the commercial potential of writing in English instead

---

* In a sample of their future enmity, Nabokov threw even this compliment back in Wilson's face: "The 'miseries, horrors and handicaps' that he assumes I was subjected to during 40 years, before we first met in New York, are mostly figments of his warped fantasy."

of Russian. Even before he departed for America in 1940, he had composed his first novel, *The Real Life of Sebastian Knight*, in English. His Russian émigré audience was disappearing, melting away to different continents. Nabokov espied his new world even before he arrived there.

Another fact: Like Wilson, Nabokov was quite a ladies' man, even something of a rake at Cambridge and in his early twenties. But after an initially shaky period, his 1925 marriage to Vera Slonim became the center of his life. Vera was Jewish, which heightened her husband's sensitivity to Europe's resurging anti-Semitism. Nabokov's mother and sister were living in Prague, which the Nazis occupied in 1938. He moved from Berlin to Paris in 1937, and saw the future of Europe all too clearly. Getting a job outside France "is a life or death question for me," he wrote to his friend Gleb Struve. "I'm simply perishing."[28] On the gossamer promise of a summer teaching position at Stanford University, Nabokov wangled an American visa for his family. They made their American landfall in New York, aboard the steamer *Champlain*, on May 26, 1940.

A few weeks later Nicolas Nabokov reached out to Edmund Wilson on behalf of his cousin. The two men corresponded and met. It was the beginning of a beautiful friendship.

2

Such Good Friends

While Wilson helped Nabokov professionally, he wasn't alone. Nabokov had excellent contacts among the Russian émigré intelligentsia who had preceded him to America. The composer Sergei Rachmaninoff had been mailing small sums of money to Nabokov in Europe, and sent over a carton of used clothing after the two men became reacquainted in New York.[1] But Wilson, a veteran editor, author, and journalist knew the ins and outs of the New York publishing scene better than almost anyone. Like the newly arrived Nabokov, he had serious financial problems, mainly related to his inability to match his perfectly decent income with his sybaritic spending. So he knew that when *The Atlantic* offered you fifty dollars for a short story, you demanded one hundred. More often than not you would get it.

Wilson commissioned reviews from Nabokov, and introduced him to the editors of *Decision* magazine, *The Yale Review* ("a dreary quarterly"), *The Atlantic Monthly, The New Yorker* ("write to Wm. Maxwell [fiction editor at *The New Yorker*] and tell him I suggested your doing so"), and *Harper's Bazaar* ("Write to Mary Louise Aswell [editor] and mention Mary [McCarthy] and

me").[2] *Atlantic* editor Edward Weeks, a Trinity-Cambridge product like Nabokov, practically swooned the first time the spritely
forty-two-year-old writer sashayed into the downstairs café of
the Boston Ritz. Nabokov acted as if he owned the place. "He
would come in in a shabby tweed coat," Weeks recalled, "trousers
bulging at the knee, but be quite the most distinguished man in
the room, with his perfectly beautiful hazel eyes, his fine brown
hair, the *élan*, the spark. . . . He just had to walk into the room and
the girls looked around."*

Weeks loved the work, too, uttering the words every writer
dreams of hearing: "We are enchanted . . . this is genius," he
wrote Nabokov after receiving a short-story submission. Wilson
also introduced Nabokov to his first American publisher, James
Laughlin, the well-born founder of New Directions books. Laughlin published Nabokov's first English-language novel, *The Real
Life of Sebastian Knight*, with a flattering blurb ("absolutely
enchanting") from Wilson. The notoriously tightfisted Laughlin,
a scion of the Pittsburgh-based Jones & Laughlin steel fortune,
tried to withhold an advance on royalties, but Nabokov—a quick-
on-the-uptake student at the Edmund Wilson Academy of Not
Taking Sh*t from Publishers—insisted on payment. He won. (The
poet Delmore Schwartz was Laughlin's reader for *Knight*.) The
book appeared eleven days after the Japanese attack on Pearl Harbor, and sank accordingly.

Laughlin and Nabokov became friends, and the latter gladly
accepted an invitation to Laughlin's ski lodge in Alta, Utah, to

---

* Wilson, by contrast, was no clotheshorse. In *Here at* The New Yorker, (1975), Brendan Gill described his colleague as "a short, overweight man in floppy dark clothes,
wearing a floppy hat and carrying a floppy briefcase—and one saw at once that of all
the languages he had mastered, dress was the language that concerned him least."

pursue his passion for butterfly collecting. Wilson also talked up
Nabokov to Random House's Robert Linscott, best known as William Faulkner's editor. Linscott filed a memorable "reader's report"
after perusing *The Person from Porlock*, which Henry Holt would
later publish as the novel *Bend Sinister*: "I first heard of [Nabo-
kov] through Edmund Wilson, who considered him the most brilliant man he has ever met," Linscott wrote. Wilson "thinks that
some day he will write one of the great contemporary novels."[3]

Wilson did much more than write letters and telephone editors
on Nabokov's behalf. He liked to socialize, and enjoyed dining,
drinking, discussing anything and everything with the Nabokovs and with his wife of the moment—the already famous, and
young, and beautiful novelist Mary McCarthy. The families spent
Thanksgiving 1941 together at Wilson's rambling Cape Cod home
in Wellfleet, the first of many meetings among the four of them.

The visit provided the occasion for Nabokov's poem "The
Refrigerator Awakes": "Crash!/And if darkness could sound, it
would sound like this giant/Waking up in the torture house, trying to die." It was the first of dozens of works that Nabokov would
place in *The New Yorker*.

After his summer at Stanford, Nabokov returned to live in
Cambridge, Massachusetts, and started teaching at Wellesley College. The two couples often entertained each other or gathered at
the spacious home of the Harvard comparative literature professor
Harry Levin, whose Latvian-born wife, Elena, was a gifted writer
and Russian translator. Often included in the mix were Wilson's
Cape Cod neighbors Paul and Nina Chavchavadze, close friends
who occasionally helped him puzzle through Russian texts.

A complex web of vestigial ties linked the couples. Nina
Chavchavadze, for instance, was born a Romanov, the great-

Undated photo of Vladimir Nabokov (*far right*) with a group of Nina Chavchavadze's friends in Cambridge, England, in the early 1920s. Of royal blood, Nina ended up living next door to Edmund Wilson on Cape Cod. *(Courtesy Sasha Chavchavadze)*

granddaughter of Czar Nicholas I, Alexander Pushkin's nemesis and tormentor.* As a young émigrée socialite in England, she had flirted with the handsome Cambridge undergraduate Vladimir Nabokov. Vera Nabokova's father, a successful businessman under the old regime, had once worked as the steward of the Chavchavadze estate. Mary McCarthy remembered Nabokov "tying himself in knots" over the prospect of meeting Nina again, although no awkwardness occurred between the easygoing Chavchavadzes and the nervous Nabokov. "Once it had happened, he relaxed," McCarthy told Nabokov's biographer Brian Boyd.

* In her memoir of life with her father, *Close to the Magician*, Rosalind Wilson remembers Nina as an occasional source of naughty tales: "Anastasia had been a very unpleasant child, pulling the wings off butterflies, *par exemple.*"

McCarthy, whom Boyd interviewed near the end of her life, recalled plenty of choice details about the "austere" and "puritanical" Nabokovs, who were living in a modestly furnished apartment in Cambridge at the time. "He was quite anti-alcohol," McCarthy recalled, "and Vera was even more prohibitionist." McCarthy, in her late twenties, was trying her best to be a housewife, which prompted some gentle mockery from Nabokov. "He made great fun of my 'lifestyle,' " as we would call it today," she said in 1985, "which included quite a number of novelties, and he hated novelties." For example, her cherries jubilee. "He was just horrified by it, he invented pseudonyms for it."

But he ate it, and enjoyed it.

Later divorced from Wilson after eight stormy years of marriage, McCarthy professed to have been "amazed" by the subsequent falling-out between her former husband and Nabokov. "They had a ball together," she told Boyd. "Edmund was always in a state of joy when Vladimir appeared, even more so at home than *chez eux.*"

In 1943 Wilson engineered a Guggenheim Fellowship* for Nabokov, who at the time was the rare laureate over the age of forty. Nabokov was temporarily out of work, and scrambling financially. The thank-you note was heartfelt: "Dear Bunny, I got that Guggenheim Fellowship. Thanks, dear friend. . . . I have noticed that whenever you are involved in any of my affairs they are always successful."

A WONDROUS BY-PRODUCT of the early years of the Wilson-Nabokov infatuation was their famous correspondence, which

---

* Wilson—presciently?—called them "Googleheims."

flourished during the 1940s and 1950s. Even during their pro-tracted feud, Nabokov expressed the hope (though not to Wilson) that their letters might someday be collected. After Nabokov's death, Vera and Elena Wilson recruited Simon Karlinsky, the University of California Slavic literature professor, to edit and annotate the letters, which were printed in two separate editions after new correspondence surfaced during the 1990s. The letters were eloquent enough to form the script for a short, two-person epistolary play, "Dear Bunny, Dear Volodya," edited by Terry Quinn and performed in selected venues, once with William F. Buckley playing Wilson and Dmitri Nabokov reading the letters written by his father.

The letters sparkle and roam over a beguilingly eclectic array of topics. With whom else could Nabokov share a bilingual play on words, in French and Russian? ("Il fait diablement chaud, ce qui n'est pas *khorochaud.*" ["It's devilishly hot, which is not good."] *Khorosho* means "good," or "okay," in Russian.) Good French meant a lot to Nabokov. He viewed it as the skeleton key to himself, and to his favorite poet. To "write about Pushkin and also about me," you must know French literature, he once remarked to Kar-linksy, who "had" French. Nabokov groused that neither Andrew Field, his first biographer, nor his friend Alfred Appel, who aspired to be his biographer, had a proper grounding in French literature.[4]

For whom else could Wilson compose a bilingual limerick, alluding to butterfly genitalia?

> *Our perverse old pisatel' [writer] Vladimir*
> *Was stroking a butterfly's femur*
> *"I prefer this," he said*
> *"To a lady in bed,*
> *Or even a velvet-eyed lemur."*

Wilson was poking fun at Nabokov's lepidopterical specialty—butterfly genitalia, which he described as "minuscule sculptural hooks, teeth, spurs, etc. . . . visible only under a microscope."*

Who else could trade amphisbaenic poems, a literary subgenre named if not invented by Wilson? The amphisbaena was a mythological serpent that had two poison-spitting heads, one at the end of its tail. So Wilson christened a stanza in which the final rhyme was an anagram of the rhyme that ended the previous line, for example:

> To the peaks of the nearest Azore
> As the sun, a dry vin rosé,
> Orange-pink, darkens the pines,
> And I startle a pair of snipe.[5]

This prompted Nabokov's response, "To E.W. on reading his amphisbaenic poem":

> At first my brain was somewhat numbed
> By your somnambulistic numbers, Edmund. . . .

For that matter, who else would read, much less write, pages upon pages about prosody, a subject on which both men considered themselves to be world-class experts? "Once and for all, you should tell yourself that in these questions of prosody—no matter what the language involved—you are wrong, and I am right, always," Nabokov wrote to Wilson in what was very much not their

---

* The website atlasobscura.com reports that Harvard's Peabody Museum has preserved Nabokov's " 'Genitalia Cabinet,' where hundreds of documents, cigar boxes crammed with butterfly penises, and dried out specimens were all labeled in Nabokov's elegant handwriting."

last word on this deadly subject. Their discussions of English and Russian prosody* could fill a book, albeit not this one. Nabokov published a small book on Russian prosody as part of his *Onegin* translation.

For the first several years of their exchanges, the two men could cheerfully disagree, for instance, on the correct pronunciation of "nihilist." (Nabokov pronounced the word "NEE-hil-ist," Wilson "NIE-i-list.") "Dear Volodya: Nihilist [NI-hilist] is pronounced the way I pronounce it—not NEE-hilist. See any dictionary."[6]

Or on the question of lovemaking in taxicabs. Can it be done, and if so, how?

Wilson had been reading one of Nabokov's Russian novels, *Mary,* in the original, and noted that the protagonists "are supposed to have had their first *étreinte* [embrace] on the floor of a taxicab. I don't think you can have had any actual experience of this kind or you would know that it is not done that way."

"My dear Bunny," Nabokov promptly replied. "It could be done, and in fact was done, in Berlin taxi-cabs, models 1920. I remember having interviewed numerous Russian taxi-drivers, fine White Russians all of them, and they all said, yes, that was the correct way. I am afraid I am quite ignorant of the American technique."[7]

In their serious exchanges about literature, Nabokov's wildly heterodox tastes and eccentric judgments quickly established themselves. Dostoyevsky was "a third-rate writer and his fame

* "That corpse of a topic," as the former Oxford Professor of Poetry Christopher Ricks calls it. Nabokov's prosodic logorrhea on this subject is ironical, because in a 1930 letter to his brother Kirill, who was writing poetry in Prague, Vladimir explained that "all the schemes of Russian poetry" can be broken down into five simple elements, which he listed in about 150 words. "As you see, this is all simple," Vladimir wrote, "and can be assimilated in five minutes." In real life Nabokov probably wrote a thousand pages on the subject.

is incomprehensible."* Nabokov called Henry James "that pale
porpoise" and viewed him as a warmed-over Turgenev manqué.
T. S. Eliot and Thomas Mann were "fakes," and when Wilson suggested that his friend include a Jane Austen novel in his Cornell
survey course on European literature, Nabokov bridled. "I dislike
Jane [Austen]," he informed Wilson, "and am prejudiced, in fact,
against all women writers." Nabokov reviled Freud, "the Viennese
wizard" or "the Viennese quack," and would later include him in
a personal rogues' gallery of four doctors to be avoided at all costs,
the other three being: Zhivago, the protagonist of the Boris Pas-
ternack novel that Nabokov hated; the international humanitar-
ian Dr. Albert Schweitzer, about whom even Wilson had his own
reservations ("can't help feeling that there is something phony
somewhere"[8]); and Fidel Castro, who had received an honorary
doctorate from Moscow University.

Wilson held strong opinions, too. His daughter, Rosalind,
remembered that, even though her father suffered a nervous
breakdown in 1929, he also harbored a healthy skepticism about
"Dr. Freud." He complained about "that sort of nerve doctor"
who treated him in the sanitarium: "He tried to get me on the
couch. But I wouldn't let him!"[9] (Wilson left a different note in
his diary: "The sanitarium was boring beyond description—no
drinking!"[10]) Likewise Wilson was no stranger to magniloquent
outbursts à la Nabokov: "I have been bored by everything about
Spain except Spanish painting," he once remarked in *The New
Yorker*. "I have made a point of learning no Spanish, and I have

---

* Nabokov even scorned Dostoyevsky's famous 1880 speech at the unveiling of
a Pushkin monument in Moscow, often credited with enshrining the poet in the
Russian literary canon. Nabokov noted that Dostoyevsky bungled some *Onegin*
facts, "which goes to show," he wrote, "that Dostoyevsky had not really read *Eugene
Onegin*."

never been able to get through *Don Quixote*. . . . I have never visited Spain or any Hispanic country."[11]

Wilson's fascination with the Russian language often wells up
in the correspondence, accompanied by playful attempts to show
off for his erudite friend. Wilson liked to include the odd Cyrillic
phrase in his letters, and Nabokov often responded with a phrase
or two of his own. Wilson's Russian isn't of mere academic interest, because when the two men set to fighting, Nabokov asserted,
forcefully, that Wilson was a hapless flounderer in the language
of Pushkin.*

To be fair, Wilson was generally aware of his Russian-language
shortcomings, but he worked hard on the language, as a hobby.
There are numerous handwritten notes and newspaper clippings
in Russian sent by Nina Chavchavadze among Wilson's papers,
and family members and friends recall the two of them poring
over Russian stories and poetry, with Nina taking Wilson by the
hand, as it were. "Nina Chavchavadze and I read Pushkin together
two or three times a week," Wilson wrote to Nabokov in 1942. "I
have just discovered how truly awful the Russian numerals are,
and it has just about killed any faint hopes I may have had about
ever learning to speak the language."[†12]

The Chavchavadze translation machine didn't always function
perfectly, either. Wilson complained in a 1943 letter to his friend

---

* For the record, Nabokov's English was hardly above reproach. The *New York
Times* reviewer of *Sebastian Knight* deemed the author's English to be "interesting in a Walt Disney kind of way." Even when the ur-Americanized *Lolita* appeared
in 1957, Vita Sackville-West opined: "I don't know what language it was originally
written in . . . it is not even bad American and is certainly not good English." Wilson
sometimes provided useful criticism of Nabokov's prose, once explaining the difference between a pun and a bon mot, for instance. "It is only occasionally that your
English goes off the track," he wrote in 1943.

† Wilson's son, Reuel, a retired professor of Slavic studies, remembers that Nina
Chavchavadze and his father generally spoke English during their tutoring sessions.
"EW's spoken French was the best," Wilson recalled. "His Russian was slow, but he
could express what he wanted to say."

Helen Muchnic, a professor of Russian literature at Smith College, that he was finding Alexander Griboyedov's classic play *Gorye ot Uma (Woe from Wit)* "appallingly difficult." He adds that he appealed to Nina Chavchavadze for help, but "she didn't understand it at all, either."[13]

That same year Wilson published one of his first ruminations on the "true horrors" of the Russian language in the *Atlantic Monthly*.[14] The five verbal aspects; the numerical dates in which every digit is separately declined; the further subdivision of the imperfective: "What, then, is one to do about Russian?" he wails. "One must observe the Russian verbs as the bird-watcher does birds, collect them as the lepidopterist does butterflies"—surely not a random metaphor.

Wilson apparently read enough of Nabokov's *Mary*, then available only in Russian, to grasp the finer points of the taxi-coupling scene. On the other hand, he freely admitted to Nabokov in a December 1940 letter, "Your *Priglasheniye na Kazn [Invitation to a Beheading]* has stumped me. I had better go back to Tolstoy til my Russian is stronger."[15] Reading Tolstoy and Gogol, as he did, in the original is no mean feat, either. Wilson made schoolboy mistakes, muddling the easily confusable words for "Sunday" and "Resurrection"—both would be transliterated *Voskreseniye*, although they are spelled differently in Russian—and occasionally muffing a participle or a verb ending, as almost all nonnative speakers do. He certainly deserved an A for effort. Wilson once sent Nabokov a six-line clerihew, in Russian, poking fun at Leo Tolstoy's pretending to be a peasant. (A clerihew is a short poetic parody, usually of four lines rhymed *aabb*.) It's not very good, and not very grammatical, and earned this scathing entry in Nabokov's private diary: "Bunny Wilson sends me a lame little epigram he wrote in hopelessly bad Russian."

After 1946 Wilson found himself living with a fluent Russian speaker, his fourth wife, Elena. Nina Chavchavadze introduced the pair. Elena was the granddaughter of the onetime Russian ambassador to Japan and the United States, and the daughter of a woman who left Russia in 1904 to marry a Prussian aristocrat. She Russified Wilson's existence, in a limited way. "Elena is quietly transforming the house so that parts of it look like Turgenev," he complained in a 1947 letter to Nabokov. Wilson addressed the introduction of his 1972 book, *A Window on Russia*, to Elena, recalling that "my Russian was so inadequate when you and I first married that when we tried to communicate in a language that other people could not understand, I spoke so very badly . . . that we were unable to understand one another."

While it is true that Nabokov occasionally derided Wilson's Russian, this is the same man who reached out to Wilson when he was looking for a translator for his most precious Russian-language creation, the novel *The Gift*. The publisher, Alfred A. Knopf, had suggested Avrahm Yarmolinsky, whose wife (and translating partner), Babette Deutsch, Nabokov would gleefully anathematize in later years. In any case, they wouldn't do. "I know of one man who could do it if I helped him with his Russian," Nabokov wrote, "but I am afraid you have other dogs to beat."[16] Wilson indeed replied that he was too busy, and that checking his uncertain Russian might present as much work as if Nabokov translated the book himself.

There is an odd artifact among Nabokov's papers—a short, newsy letter from Wilson, written entirely in Russian.[17] It is brief and chatty, written at about the level of an accomplished second-year language student. Wilson muffs a preposition when alluding to his forthcoming book *Patriotic Gore*. Otherwise his penmanship is excellent and his grammar is functional. In most classes, he would earn a solid B+.

The early letters also tease out a delicate issue: Wilson's opinion of Nabokov's writing. In 1941 Laughlin sent Wilson the proofs of *The Real Life of Sebastian Knight,* and as he testified in his blurb, he loved it. "The whole book is brilliantly and beautifully done," Wilson wrote to Nabokov. "You and Conrad must be the only examples of foreigners succeeding in English in this field."

The next novel, *Bend Sinister,* presented a problem. Wilson didn't like it ("I was rather disappointed") and told Nabokov as much in a long January 1947 letter. He thought the book was slow: "It doesn't move with the Pushkinian rapidity that I have always admired in your writing." More important, he thought Nabokov's fictional account of life in a soul-crushing dictatorship rang false. "You aren't good at this kind of subject," Wilson commented, "which involves questions of politics and social change, because you are totally uninterested in these matters and have never taken the trouble to understand them."

Having said that, Wilson kept his feelings to himself, and talked the book up to his friend Allen Tate, an editor at Henry Holt, which published *Sinister* that same year. Nabokov had hoped for a different reaction, and Simon Karlinsky thought Wilson's lack of enthusiasm evinced a "crack" in the men's relationship. He may have been right. A small academic subculture has sprung up to prove that *Sinister* has elements of a tribute to Wilson, and that many of the two men's heated debates, for example, over Shakespeare's use of iambs, found their way verbatim into the text.[18] Nabokov clearly thought Wilson had missed the point of the book, and had missed the subtle allusions to their friendship. One year after publication he wrote to Wilson about *Sinister,* "You should read it someday."[19]

Wilson loved Nabokov's next book, *Conclusive Evidence,* the childhood memoir that would later be republished as *Speak, Memory.* "The English of *Conclusive Evidence* is at least as good as Conrad's," Wilson wrote to Nabokov, "and has qualities that Conrad could never have managed."[20]

These were private comments. Although he did sometimes review books by friends of his—for example, the novelist Dawn Powell and his Princeton classmate, the poet John Peale Bishop— it did not go unnoticed that Wilson never reviewed a book by Nabokov during the first quarter century of their friendship. Elena Levin noticed, and thought that it rankled Nabokov.[21] Wilson often made noises about writing an overview of Nabokov. For instance, in 1952 he told Vera that "the time is approaching when I am going to read [Vladimir's] complete works and write an essay on them that will somewhat annoy him."[22] But the promised *tour d'horizon* never materialized.

When the Nabokov-Wilson imbroglio boiled over in 1965, Nabokov archly observed that "I have always been grateful to him for the tact he showed in refraining from reviewing any of my novels." By that time Nabokov was flush with cash and internationally famous as the author of *Lolita,* one of the best-selling books in the world. It was strictly speaking true that Wilson had not reviewed a Nabokov novel, but he did review Nabokov's eccentric critique of Nikolai Gogol,* his second submission to

---

* How eccentric? Pretty darned eccentric. A brief (174 pages) "Life and Work" overview of one of Nabokov's favorite writers, the book began with Gogol's death, ended with his birth, and was liberally padded with long excerpts from Gogol's work. Typical commentary: "The plot of 'The Government Inspector' is as unimportant as the plots of all Gogol books." The final chapter, 6, re-creates an exchange between the author and his publisher, Laughlin, "in Utah, sitting in the lounge of an Alpine hotel." Laughlin is badgering Nabokov to tell the reader what Gogol's books are

Laughlin's fledgling New Directions publishing house, for *The New Yorker.*

The review says pretty much everything Wilson thought about Nabokov's writing, with no punch pulled. The praise was sincere. "Mr. Nabokov . . . is a novelist of the non-realistic sort, and he has written the kind of book which can only be written by one artist about another—an essay which takes its place with the very small body of first-rate criticism of Russian literature in English."

The criticism was equally direct. "His puns are particularly awful," and "the reader is also annoyed by the frequent self-indulgence of the author in poses, perversities and vanities . . . and, along with them, a kind of yapping and snarling in principle at everything connected with the Russian Revolution that sometimes throws the baby out with the blood bath."[23]

When he reprinted the review in a 1950 collection, Wilson added one final line that he must have known would irk Nabokov: "In spite of some errors, Mr. Nabokov's mastery of English almost rivals Joseph Conrad's."

Enough with the Conrad already! Nabokov hated the all-too-frequent comparisons with Conrad, who achieved worldwide fame in English, his second language. Conrad, born Józef Teodor Konrad Korzeniowski, was a Polish seafarer who began his literary career at age thirty-eight, writing in English. Nabokov complained to Wilson about the last line of the Gogol review: "Conrad knew how to handle readymade English better than I, but I know better the other kind."[24] In an interview with the *New York Times* not long

---

about: "I have gone through it carefully, and so has my wife, and we have not found the plots." Nabokov tells the reader that he tacked on a seven-page chronology, with plot summaries, to placate Laughlin. Clearly he thought Laughlin wouldn't read the addendum, because he inserted this random sentence into the recitation of Gogol's life: "Browning's door is preserved in the library of Wellesley College." [It is.] The Robert Browning "Easter egg"—computer lingo for a hidden joke—survived the 1959 and 1961 reeditions of *Nikolai Gogol,* but later vanished from the text.

after, Nabokov elaborated on his disdain for Conrad: "It irritates me a little when people compare me to Conrad," he explained.

Naturally I am not at all displeased in a literary way; that isn't what I mean. The point is Conrad had never been a Polish writer, he started right in as an English writer. I had had a number of books in Russian before I wrote in English. My books were completely banned in Russia and circulated among the Russian émigrés only. There were millions of them.[25]

Translation: I am a far more accomplished writer than Conrad. In 1967, when he was internationally famous, Nabokov let his hair down in a *Playboy* interview: "I cannot abide Conrad's souvenir-shop style, and bottled ships, and shell necklaces of romanticist clichés."* Another trespass: Nabokov would have known that Conrad had praised the work of the famous Russian-to-English translator Constance Garnett, one of Nabokov's bêtes noires. ("I can do nothing with Constance Garnett's dry shit," he lamented to his publisher Laughlin while puzzling through her version of Gogol's play *The Government Inspector*.)

Nabokov might have admired Conrad more had he known that the Anglicized Pole shared his disdain for Fyodor Dostoyevsky. "[Conrad] hated him because he was Russian, because he was mad, and because he was confused," the Spanish novelist and critic Javier Marias notes in *Written Lives*, "and the mere mention of his name would provoke a furious outburst."

---

* Wilson's attitude toward Conrad was: Invoke him, yes; read him, no. He could never stand *Nostromo*, his upstate New York friend Richard Hauer Costa wrote in *Edmund Wilson, Our Neighbor from Talcottville:* "Then he broke into a tirade against Conrad generally, even *Lord Jim*, another book he had tried and failed with."

ANDREW FIELD, who spent years with Nabokov researching a snakebit biography, says the letters to Wilson represent Nabokov's "most protracted and voluminous" correspondence.[26] The two men were unashamedly intimate companions. "You are one of the very few people in the world whom I keenly miss when I do not see them," Nabokov wrote to Wilson in 1948, returning a borrowed pair of socks.[27]

Their early years together had elements of a courtship, thriving on shared discoveries. Nabokov once even tried to jolly Wilson into sampling butterfly collecting: "Try, Bunny," he wrote. Collecting butterflies "is the noblest sport in the world." They savored the dialectic of conflicting opinions, but they had many traits in common, too. Neither man could drive. Nabokov must have noticed, and envied, Wilson's notorious preprinted kiss-off note ("Edmund Wilson regrets that it is impossible for him to: Read Manuscripts . . . Broadcast or Appear on Television . . . Take Part in Writers' Congresses . . . Autograph Books for Strangers,"), which gained a certain renown in twentieth-century American letters. He eventually drafted his own version: "Vladimir Nabokov finds it impossible to answer all the kind letters he receives from his readers. He extends his warmest thanks to the many friends and strangers who send him . . ."

"I was sometimes in doubt as to what kind of role I wanted to play," Wilson wrote near the end of his life, but "I have never had much real doubt about who or what I was."[28] The same words apply to Vladimir Nabokov.

Both men also shared a pointed disdain for the professorate and its Pecksniffian sensibilities. Nabokov and Wilson each wrote

I don't give readings either unless I am offered a very large fee.

EDMUND WILSON REGRETS THAT IT IS IMPOSSIBLE FOR HIM TO:

READ MANUSCRIPTS,

WRITE ARTICLES OR BOOKS TO ORDER,

WRITE FOREWORDS OR INTRODUCTIONS,

MAKE STATEMENTS FOR PUBLICITY PURPOSES,

DO ANY KIND OF EDITORIAL WORK,

JUDGE LITERARY CONTESTS,

GIVE INTERVIEWS,

CONDUCT EDUCATIONAL COURSES,

DELIVER LECTURES,

GIVE TALKS OR MAKE SPEECHES,

BROADCAST OR APPEAR ON TELEVISION,

TAKE PART IN WRITERS' CONGRESSES,

ANSWER QUESTIONNAIRES,

CONTRIBUTE TO OR TAKE PART IN *fee.* SYMPOSIUMS OR "PANELS" OF *E W* ANY KIND,

CONTRIBUTE MANUSCRIPTS FOR SALES,

DONATE COPIES OF HIS BOOKS TO LIBRARIES,

AUTOGRAPH BOOKS FOR STRANGERS,

ALLOW HIS NAME TO BE USED ON LETTERHEADS,

SUPPLY PERSONAL INFORMATION ABOUT HIMSELF,

SUPPLY PHOTOGRAPHS OF HIMSELF,

SUPPLY OPINIONS ON LITERARY OR OTHER SUBJECTS.

"Edmund Wilson regrets . . ." Perhaps the most infamous three-by-five-inch card in twentieth-century American literature. *(Private collection)*

nasty attacks on the academy, Nabokov in his 930-page *Onegin* "Commentary" and in the novel *Pale Fire*. Wilson took immense delight in pasquinading the Modern Language Association, the academic ossuary for literary pleasure. ("It publishes a periodical . . . which contains for the most part unreadable articles on literary problems of very minute or no interest."[29]) At the same time, both men kept a Willie Sutton–like eye trained on American universities: That's where the money was. Nabokov toiled in the academic vineyards for almost two decades, including eleven years as a distinguished professor at Cornell. Wilson, who was neither a good teacher nor a good lecturer, eagerly pursued the top-dollar honoraria occasionally proffered by status-seeking colleges and universities.

For many years Wilson and Nabokov could ask each other almost anything. Just two years into their friendship, Wilson inquired if he might be able to take over Nabokov's teaching slot at Wellesley College because a promised visiting professorship at Cornell had fallen through. Nabokov diplomatically answered, no, it's *my* job.[30] A few years later Nabokov broached a similar request ("I should not like to seem to be butting into your own arrangements in *any* way . . ."): Could he cover books for *The New Yorker* when Wilson went on leave? Wilson talked to editor William Shawn, who said he had already penciled in other editors for what Nabokov called "the inter-Wilsonian gaps."[31]

Nabokov was duly grateful for Wilson's entrée into *The New Yorker*, which not only brought his work to a large and sophisticated audience but also paid well. Nabokov liked the magazine and especially liked his fiction editor, Katharine White. But early in his tenure with the magazine, "a man called Ross started to 'edit' " one of his stories, "and I wrote to Mrs. White telling her that I could not accept any of those ridiculous and exasperating alterations."[32] Harold Ross, who was the magazine's founder and editor in chief, yielded considerable ground during this dustup after Nabokov threatened to take back his story.

Aware of the magazine's longing to "iron out" Nabokov's prose, Wilson sent White a very long letter not only defending his friend's idiosyncratic style ("How *can* you people say it is overwritten?") but also attacking the magazine's penchant for publishing prissy prose. Nabokov's story could only seem overwritten "in contrast with the pointless and inane little anecdotes that are turned out by the *New Yorker's* processing mill and that the reader forgets two minutes after he reads them—if, indeed, he has even paid attention, at the time his eye was slipping down the column, to what he was reading about."

Wilson went on to deride "the *New Yorker*'s idea of style" generally. "The editors are so afraid of anything that is unusual, that is not expected, that they put a premium on insipidity and banality."[33] It was a generous gesture, and both Wilson and Nabokov contributed to the magazine for another quarter century.*

Wilson loved magic and liked to perform tricks for small children. His eldest daughter titled her memoir of life with him *Near the Magician*. Nabokov was likewise obsessed with sleight of hand and prestidigitation, most especially in literature, in making things not as they seem. It's hard to think of a Nabokov creation that isn't a trick, or a puzzle to be worked out. There is his famous foreword to *The Gift*, in which he begs the readers of this most autobiographical of novels about Russian émigrés in Germany "not to confuse the designer with the design." Or the equally well-known *Lolita* afterword, where he writes that "any comments coming straight from me may strike one—may strike me, in fact—as an impersonation of Vladimir Nabokov talking about his own book." Nabokov is the man who preferred to put quotation marks around the word "reality," for good reason.[34]

When his mother died in 1951, Wilson inherited a sprawling, beloved old stone house in upstate Talcottville, New York. He had read that one of Casanova's mistresses memorialized their relationship by etching their names on a windowpane with a diamond. In a stairway of the Talcottville house, Wilson had windowpanes

---

* Wilson shared Nabokov's *noli mi tangere* attitude toward *New Yorker* editing, as his longtime colleague E. J. Kahn recalled in *About* The New Yorker *and Me*: "Edmund Wilson is reputed to have stipulated before agreeing to contribute to *The New Yorker* that his prose was sacrosanct and was not to be changed by so much as a comma. (I can believe that story even if it isn't true: Wilson-in-print could have stood some pruning, just as some muting might have made more tolerable the shrill stabbing voice of Wilson-in-person, which, whenever the great man approached to within about a hundred feet of where anybody else was trying to think, murdered cerebration.)"

engraved with etched messages from his many famous friends. Using a diamond-pointed pencil, Wilson's guests W. H. Auden, Stephen Spender, Dorothy Parker, and the French poet-diplomat Saint-John Perse (Alexis Leger), among others, etched messages for posterity. Nabokov left a brief rhyme in Russian: "There are nights when as soon as I lie down/My bed sails off to Russia."

In a beautiful passage from his 1972 memoir, *Upstate*, Wilson recalled that "the pane with the Nabokov poem on the upstairs door to the balcony came out in a beautiful way against the pink background at dawn, looking like a pattern of frost. I called up Volodya and told him this and he came back with one of his inescapable puns: 'There is an English word for that: rime.' "[35]

ON MAY 25, 1957, a friend drove Wilson from Talcottville to Ithaca, New York, to visit the Nabokovs. It was an interesting moment in the hosts' lives. *Lolita* had appeared in Paris, published in English by Maurice Girodias's pornography-dabbling Olympia Press. It had achieved a succès de scandale, but not much else, as both England and America had banned its importation. Wilson had read the original manuscript and disliked it. He could comfortably assume that *Lolita* would fizzle in Europe, where louche books enjoyed a modest half-life, sputtered, and died. There seemed to be little chance that an American publisher would risk a lawsuit and publish a comedy about pedophilia.

At the same time Nabokov was very close to finishing his translation of *Eugene Onegin*, a sleek little vehicle with a Winnebago-size appendage in tow—the vast, unwieldy 930-page "Commentary." That, too, could be safely assumed to be box-office death. Who would publish, much less buy, Nabokov's over-stuffed white elephant? He had shown portions of the manuscript to Wilson, who told Helen Muchnic that "the translation is good, I think. He has more or less accepted my method, in the passages I translated, of following the text exactly and writing lines of irregular length, with a metrical base of iambic pentameter."

This alludes to an *Onegin* stanza that Wilson translated in his *1936 New Republic* article, "In Honor of Pushkin." Nabokov saw the essay in Wilson's 1948 collection, *The Triple Thinkers*, and indeed credited Wilson as "the first to have adopted unrhymed iambics for rendering *EO*." Nabokov then pointed out numerous inaccuracies in Wilson's stanza when *Onegin* came out in 1964.

During this stay Nabokov challenged Wilson to read aloud from the Russian text of *Onegin*. The result was disastrous. Wilson botched the very first line, improperly stressing the Russian word for "uncle," reading "dya-DYA" for "DYA-dya."[36] Nabokov would later recall that Wilson's "rather endearing little barks . . . soon had us both in stitches." But when he later chose to recollect that shared moment, neither man was in a laughing mood.

The two-day visit had the inevitable ups and downs. Wilson reported that the kerfuffle in Paris over *Lolita*, and the warm reception of the short novel *Pnin*, serialized in *The New Yorker*, had lifted Nabokov's spirits. As did a copy of *L'Histoire d'O*, the French erotic novel that Wilson had brought along as a house present. "He agreed with me," Wilson recorded in his journal, "that, trashy though it is, it exercises a certain hypnotic effect." Vera Nabokova frowned on the two men's tittering enjoyment of *nyeprilichnaya literatura* ("indecent literature") and made sure that Wilson took the book with him when he left. During the visit Wilson and Vera embarked on a lengthy dispute about the meaning of the French adjective *fastidieux*, which Wilson correctly insisted meant "tiresome" or "boring," and not "fastidious." This battle about nothing lingered in the correspondence for several weeks.

In his journal, Wilson wrote, "I always enjoy seeing them," and added a demurrer: "But there is also something in him rather nasty—the cruelty of the arrogant rich man—that makes him want to humiliate others, and his characters he has completely at his mercy."

3

Sex Doesn't Sell . . . Or Does It?

In 1946 Edmund Wilson published his second novel, *Memoirs of Hecate County*. Like a much more successful "sexy" novel that would appear roughly a decade later, *Hecate*—a collection of eight related stories, several of them quite long—had some eloquent descriptive passages, and some downright baffling parts. "Mr. and Mrs. Blackburn at Home," for instance, included an eight-page block of text in untranslated French. But, as it would be for the still-aborning *Lolita*, readers did not seize on *Hecate* for the innovative character sketches or for the intriguing digressions into French prose. Readers flocked to it for the sex.

Mainstream literary mores after World War II differed immensely from what they are today. We are condemned to live forever inside the old Cole Porter song: "Anything Goes." In Wilson's time a glimpse of stocking—or in the case of *Hecate*, a flash of a woman's "mossy damp underparts"—was awfully shocking. As he was to discover, anything did *not* go.

Hecate, which Wilson called his "favorite among my books— I have never understood why the people who interest themselves in my work never pay any attention to it," has not stood the test of time. Even Wilson's friends thought he was a programmatic novelist, meaning that his fiction seemed to be trying to prove something, or to be illustrating a theory rather than telling a story. (One could level that same criticism at much of Nabokov's fiction.) The scandalous sex scenes now seem like a glimpse of a naughty picture in a turn-of-the-previous-century stereoscope. Of archaeological interest, and not much more.

When *Hecate*'s protagonist finally beds "The Princess with the Golden Hair," in one of the stories, he writes that her nude body

> . . . did really resemble a Venus. Not only were her thighs perfect columns, but all that lay between them was impressively beautiful, too, with an aesthetic value that I had never found there before. The mount was of a classical femininity: round and smooth and plump; the fleece, if not quite golden, was blond and curly and soft, and the portals were a deep tender rose.

And so on. What is curious is that in between the isolated and brief episodes of lovemaking, the protagonist holds forth on any number of subjects not guaranteed to entrance young ladies. The narrator, a thinly disguised Edmund Wilson, regales the working girl, Anna, with lectures on the Russian Revolution and the role of the proletariat in a capitalist society. He woos Imogen, the golden-tressed, stay-at-home suburbanite, with talk "about Goya and his queer imagination and his affair with the duchess of Alba."

"You talk so brilliantly," Imogen tells our hero. "You're really a brilliant man, aren't you?" These must have been words that Wilson had heard during amorous encounters, and we know from his own pen that he loved to run his mouth at inopportune moments. In his journal *The Forties*, he recalls questioning a French whore in London at such tedious length that "she finally got out her knitting."[1]

Hecate got bad reviews. "It is not a good book," Alfred Kazin told *Partisan Review* readers. Cyril Connolly, whom Wilson considered a friend, wrote that the author's sexual "descriptions, mechanistic and almost without eroticism, achieve a kind of insect monotony."[2] *The New York Times* ignored the novel; Wilson learned that the higher-ups had spiked a favorable review.[3] Years later Wilson's *New Yorker* colleague John Updike, no stranger to lubricious prose, wrote that "there was something dogged and humorless about Wilson's rendition of love; the adjective 'meaty' recurs."*

Nabokov called the book "wonderful," and claimed to have read it in one sitting. (Wilson had told him that he appeared in a tiny cameo in one of the stories, as "the clever Russian novelist" who may have known Mr. Chernokhvostov, "Mr. Blacktail," possibly the Devil, in Europe.) He was not the only reader—Alice B. Toklas was another—to detect an undercurrent of tortured Puritanism in the sexual encounters. "The reader . . . derives no kick from the hero's love-making," he wrote to Wilson. "I should have as soon tried to open a sardine can with my penis. The result is remarkably chaste, despite the frankness."†

When Nabokov unleashed a shot like this he knew to expect a return volley, with plenty of pace. "You sound as if I had made an unsuccessful attempt to write something like *Fanny Hill*,"

---

* That was the mature John Updike opining. As a fourteen-year-old boy, Updike checked *Hecate* out of the Reading, Pennsylvania, public library and savored the gamey bits, his "first and . . . most vivid glimpse of sex through the window of fiction." Similarly, teens in the 1960s pawed through *Rabbit, Run* and *Couples*, hunting for the "good parts."

† In his memoir, *To the Life of the Silver Harbor*, Wilson's son, Reuel, recalled the odd sex advice that his father dispensed: "The sole purpose of love, he pontificated, was marriage and children. Like his Puritan ancestors, and his idol, Leo Tolstoy, my father maintained that the aim of sex was procreation, not recreation." Reuel knew that this was high Polonian poppycock, and had nothing to do with the way Edmund had chosen to live his life.

Wilson answered. "The frozen and unsatisfactory character of the sexual relations is a very important part of the central theme of the book—indicated by the title—which I'm not sure that you have grasped."[4]

The intellectuals caviled, but the public didn't. The book sold fifty thousand copies in its first few months of publication, swelling Wilson's perennially depleted coffers. It also made him much more famous. He was already *New Yorker–New Republic* famous, well known to discriminating readers. Now he was national-best seller famous, with a book alternately hailed and denounced in newspapers across the country. "I'm making no end of money," he wrote to a friend in May 1946.[5] In a different letter he said, "I am counting on my new public of sex maniacs to buy 100,000 copies."[6]

But Wilson and money were never destined to share a taxicab. Not in 1946, and not ever. The powerful newspaper publisher William Randolph Hearst had embarked on a campaign against "indecent books," attempting to mobilize Catholic readers, and Catholic officeholders, against novels like *Hecate County*. In July the New York City police, acting at the behest of the Anti-Vice Society, a cat's-paw of Hearst and New York's Cardinal Francis Spellman, seized 130 copies of the book. Wilson's publisher, Doubleday, obtained a restraining order, and Wilson's friend John Dos Passos organized a committee to support his former comrade's First Amendment rights. The hoo-ha galvanized sales, which eventually totaled sixty thousand copies. In the fall Wilson burst in on his friend, the poet Louise Bogan, calling for her very finest brandy, explaining that "I am so rich and have the gout." He confided to Bogan that Doubleday would probably lose its court case against the Anti-Vice Society, and that he wouldn't be rich for long.

He was right. The sex maniacs would have to wait. In October 1946, despite eloquent testimony on Wilson's behalf by the literary critic Lionel Trilling and others, New York's Court of Special Sessions banned the sale of *Hecate*. An appeals court affirmed the decision. Wilson was out of the chips. The ruling "is an awful nuisance and is putting a crimp in my income," he informed Nabokov.[7] The case found its way to the Supreme Court, which deadlocked 4:4 on the obscenity question, with Wilson's friend Associate Justice Felix Frankfurter recusing himself from the case. Wilson was irate, and complained to a friend that "Felix was an old faker and that [he] never wanted to see him again."[8]

Quod scriptum, scriptum est. What had been written, was written. Wilson used the cash haul from *Hecate* to finance a lengthy stay in Reno, Nevada, for himself and his future (fourth) wife, Elena Mumm Thornton. The marriage would be his most successful and last until the end of his life.

LOLITA HAD a complicated genesis, which involved Wilson in several different ways.

Nabokov had addressed the subject of young-girl love in a 1939 not-short story, "The Enchanter," written in Russian in Paris and never published. (Deep-dish Nabokovians know that the author teased the "Enchanter" plot in a brief passage of *The Gift*.) Nabokov supposedly lost "The Enchanter" in his move from Europe to the United States, then found the manuscript, which he deemed unfit for publication, in 1959. In a 1947 letter to Wilson, Nabokov mentioned that he was working on two projects, a "new type of autobiography," the future *Speak, Memory*, and "a short novel about a man who liked little girls—and it's going to be called *The*

Kingdom by the Sea."[9] That was a preliminary title. Eventually he called it *Lolita*.

Nabokov mentioned the book twice again to Wilson. "In an atmosphere of great secrecy," he wrote from a summer butterfly-collecting trip in Oregon, "I shall show you—when I return east—an amazing book that will be quite ready by [the fall of 1954]." A few months later he promised Wilson that "quite soon, I may show you a monster," meaning *Lolita*.[10]

Approaching this theme for the second (or third) time while working on other book projects, including the massive *Onegin* translation and research, and teaching a full course load at Cornell, Nabokov took seven or eight years to write *Lolita*. The novel emerged as a far more sophisticated work of fiction than "The Enchanter," which Dmitri Nabokov published as a novella after his father's death. For instance, there are no named characters in "The Enchanter," just "the man," "the widow," "the girl," and so on. No nefarious Clare Quilty, no rootless and bootless Humbert Humbert, no mixedly motivated Charlotte Haze, and of course no All-American gal, Ms. Dolores "Lolita" Haze-Schiller herself.

In June 1948, as part of their occasional, comradely exchange of erotic literature, Wilson sent Nabokov a 106-page document, "Confession Sexuelle d'un Russe du Sud," which the psychologist Havelock Ellis had appended to the sixth volume of the French edition of his *Studies of Sexual Psychology*. Deemed to be an authentic document, the memoir recounted the sexual odyssey of a young, wealthy Ukrainian who lost his virginity at the age of twelve, having been seduced both by girls his age and by older women. Knocked off the path of conventional education by his sexual compulsion, the narrator rights himself as a young man and obtains an engineering degree and a respectable fiancée in

Italy. Alas, during a business trip, fate conspires to introduce him to Naples' worldly and aggressive corps of teenage prostitutes. He becomes addicted to their services, succumbs to the compulsions of his youth, and sees his marital prospects disappear. The confession ends on a note of despair: "He sees no hope of ever mastering his drives in the future," according to Simon Karlinsky, who researched the Ellis connection in detail.[11]

We know that Nabokov read the Ellis tale closely, because he referred to it twice, once in *Speak, Memory* and a second time, in greater detail, when he translated and reedited *Speak, Memory* as *Drugiye Berega* [*Other Shores*], into Russian.

While noting that Nabokov had already mentioned the *Lolita* project in 1947, Karlinksy writes that "Nabokov's reading in June 1948 of the nymphet hunter's confession published by Havelock Ellis may well have provided the additional stimulus for the next stage of the book's development."[12] Wilson clearly thought he had exerted a gravitational pull on *Lolita*'s long trajectory from notion to novel. There is, for instance, this undated letter in his Yale archive:

> Dear Volodya,
>   It lately occurred to me that I have not been sending you the *nyeprilichnuyu literaturu* ["indecent literature," written in Russian] with which I used to supply you, *and which no doubt inspired Lolita*, so I am enclosing this in my Christmas packet." [Emphasis added]*

---

* In his book *Literary Rivals* the author Richard Bradford floats the idea that *Lolita* is a complicated parody-cum-putdown of Wilson's *Hecate County*. As evidence, he notes that Humbert Humbert's first lover was named Annabel, and that Annabel sounds a lot like Anna, the protagonist's (that is, Wilson's) working-class lover in *Hecate County*. Wilson recognized the parody, Bradford writes, and "it was the cause of the end of their friendship." In a word, no.

Nabokov had finished *Lolita* by the summer of 1954. He was eager for Wilson to like it. "I consider this novel to be my best thing in English," he wrote to Wilson, "and though the theme and situation are decidedly sensuous, its art is pure and its fun riotous. I would love you to glance at it some time."[13] In that letter he mentioned that two American publishers had already turned the book down.

Wilson of course agreed to look at the manuscript, and Nabokov waited anxiously for his feedback. His fortunes had sunk yet again. Not a man given to self-pity, he described himself "in a pitiful state of destitution and debt." Their common friend Harry Levin recalled that Wilson telephoned Nabokov in Ithaca during this period, prompting the latter to expect enthusiastic comments about his new novel. False alarm! A complicated-looking moth had flown into Wilson's house, and he wanted Nabokov's help in identifying it.[14]

Wilson did read *Lolita*, sort of. The manuscript reached him in two black binders, and he read the first half. He didn't feel compelled to read more. "I like it less than anything else of yours that I have read," he wrote Nabokov, continuing:

> The short story that it grew out of was interesting, but I don't think the subject can stand this extended treatment. Nasty subjects may make fine books, but I don't feel you have got away with this. It isn't merely that the characters and the situation are repulsive in themselves, but that, presented on this scale, they seem quite unreal.[15]

That was America's leading literary tastemaker speaking ex cathedra. He must have known how desperately Nabokov wanted *Lolita* feedback, so he included two additional reviews in his let-

ter: a terse, disapproving note from his ex-wife Mary McCarthy
("I thought the writing was terribly sloppy throughout"), and
an elegant, short appreciation from his current wife, Elena. "The
little girl seems very real and accurate and her attractiveness and
seductiveness are absolutely plausible," Elena wrote. "I don't see
why the novel should be any more shocking than all the com-
monplace 'études of other unpleasant moeurs.'" She concluded:
"I couldn't put the book down and think it is very important."*

In his letter Wilson reminded his erstwhile collaborator that
Doubleday had forgiven them a fifteen-hundred-dollar advance
for a never-delivered overview of Russian literature, and might
be willing to accept this novel in its place. He also mentioned that
their friend, the Doubleday editor Jason Epstein, had just launched
the Anchor series of quality paperbacks, which might want to print
the *Onegin* project. (Nabokov called Doubleday "day-day" . . . of
course.)

Epstein remembers the back-and-forth over *Lolita*. "I was visiting Wilson, and he handed me these two black binders, which were
the manuscript for *Lolita*," he recalls. "Wilson told me, 'Vladimir
doesn't want anyone to know that he wrote this. I found it repul-
sive, but you won't.'" Wilson was right. "I found it to be very
amusing," Epstein says. He tried to get the book published at Doubleday, but the house's chief executive, Douglas Black, had spent
sixty thousand dollars in legal fees defending *Hecate County*, and

---

* The self-effacing Elena Wilson is something of a cipher, known to us mainly
through Wilson's diaries, where he documents their lovemakings, their quarrels, and
their occasional European jaunts. Her reaction to *Lolita* suggests that she had refined
literary tastes, and indeed Wilson often praises her judgment in his journals. Aside
from a brief, elegant exchange of letters with Vera Nabokova after their husbands'
deaths, little of her writing survives. The exception is a six-thousand-word unpublished manuscript, "My View From the Other Window," primarily describing her
life at Wilson's Talcottville manse, which she loathed. It's a well-written, occasionally too-candid ("Edmund . . . would be sitting on the front porch drunk in the early
sunshine") portrait of life with the Great Man.

wasn't eager to get back in the ring with the Catholic bluenoses. "I was angry that they turned it down," Epstein says. "It was one of the reasons that I left the company."*

Lolita's tortured publishing history has been widely documented. Stymied in the United States and desperate for cash, Nabokov allowed his European agent to sell the manuscript to Maurice Girodias's Olympia Press in Paris, best known for publishing avant-garde manuscripts, pornography, and combinations thereof, for example, William S. Burroughs's *Naked Lunch* and J. P. Donleavy's *The Ginger Man*. That was in 1955. In a year-end review for London's *Sunday Times*, Graham Greene pronounced *Lolita* one of the best books of the year. Conveniently, the editor of the popular *Sunday Express* tabloid declared *Lolita* to be "the filthiest book I have ever read" and "sheer unrestrained pornography." Almost overnight the book became an international public sensation. British customs banned importation of the Olympia edition, and then France banned publication altogether.

Well before the book crossed the Atlantic, *The New York Times* took favorable notice of its travails. "[*Lolita*] shocks because it is great art, because it tells a story in a wholly original way," is an anonymous reader's comment that Harvey Breit recycled into his "In and Out of Books" column. Breit noted bemusedly that his informants were comparing Nabokov to Nathanael West, Fitzgerald, Proust, and Dostoyevsky: "Not a real best-seller among them—so to hell with it." That was in March 1956. G. P. Putnam & Sons then decided that Nabokov's young protégée might be ready for her American debut. They went to press in August 1958, and

---

* Editorial committees all over America were cold-shouldering "Lo." Wilson's daughter Rosalind, who worked at the Boston publisher Houghton Mifflin, was in the room when "Jack Leggett . . . asked at an editorial meeting if we would like to see a book by Nabokov about an older man in love with a young girl. We all said no."

Lolita rivaled *Gone with the Wind* for unprecedented sales volatility. Putnam sold one hundred thousand hardcover copies in three weeks.

Although *Lolita* was battling heavy weather in the Old World, the United States had moved on from the days when conservative Catholic publicists could pillory "indecent" books. Much-banned books such as James Joyce's *Ulysses* and D. H. Lawrence's *Lady Chatterley's Lover*, were finding their way, legally, into bookstores. The Supreme Court had recently struck down a Michigan book-banning ordinance. Ironically it was Wilson's erstwhile friend Felix Frankfurter who opined that for Michigan to outlaw adult books that might hypothetically fall into the hands of children was "to burn the house to roast the pig." What seemed provocative in 1946 was just another stop on America's vicarious bed-hop in 1958. Grace Metalious had relocated Hecate County to rock-ribbed New Hampshire, selling one hundred thousand hardcover copies of her steamy best seller, *Peyton Place*. Furthermore, *Lolita* was high art; Graham Greene, Iris Murdoch, Stephen Spender, and any number of equally acculturated worthies said so.[16]

I doubt anyone would have told Wilson this, and I doubt he would have acknowledged it, but *Lolita* was a far better book than *Hecate County*. It was better written, better plotted, and, in parts, hilarious. ("Ladies and gentlemen of the jury . . . we are not sex fiends!") The novel laughed with itself and poked fun at itself with a gossamer irony that simply wasn't in Wilson's literary tool kit.

Hurricane *Lolita* (from *Pale Fire*, ll. 679–680: "It was a year of tempests, Hurricane / Lolita swept from Florida to Maine") swept across Europe, America, and the world, changing the Nabokovs' lives forever, and inevitably changing their relations with Edmund Wilson. Wilson acknowledged to Nabokov that the "rampancy of *Lolita* . . . seems to have opened the door to other wantons," meaning that *Hecate County* would reappear in 1959.[17] But it flopped, and *Lolita* continued to soar, over new countries and over new continents. Wilson could be forgiven for thinking: There but for the errant grace of God go I.

4

---∞∞---

Whose Mother Is Russia Anyway?

Lolita dominated the American best-seller lists well into the fall, until Boris Pasternak's *Doctor Zhivago* displaced it at the number-one spot on the fiction list. Both books lingered near the top of the list for more than a year, creating yet another curious battleground for Nabokov the novelist and Wilson the critic.

Nabokov and Pasternak knew about each other. Russian literature was too small a playing field, and their talents were too large, for them to be strangers. Nabokov often hailed Pasternak as a great poet, "a kind of masculine Emily Dickinson," albeit one whose style had some rough edges. When the first manuscripts of *Doctor Zhivago* surfaced in the West, a friend suggested the ideal translator to Pasternak: "a poet, who is completely bilingual: Vladimir Nabokov." "That won't work," Pasternak replied. "He's too jealous of my wretched position in this country to do it properly."[1]

That is a hard comment to parse, because Pasternak had been suffering from censorship and torment through the decades of Joseph Stalin's rule. He may have had an insight that almost no one shared: that Nabokov would have traded places with him, just to replant his roots in Russian soil.

Nabokov's conduct vis-à-vis Pasternak and *Zhivago* was erratic and disgraceful. Aesthetically, he didn't like the book. One could argue that it was a big, sprawling mess, chronicling the stories of storm-tossed characters pinballing around the canvas of early-twentieth-century Russian and Soviet history. Dr. Yuri Zhivago is a poet hiding from history; his mistress, Lara, is the ineffable soul of Russia; Strelnikov is the self-invented servant of the dialectic; Victor Komarovsky, memorably played by Rod Steiger in the David Lean movie, is a Dostoyevskian titan of evil and manipulation—or is he? It's a wonderful melodrama about events that Nabokov couldn't stand to see distorted and stylized. He thought the book was a saccharine, jerry-built overview of a period of Soviet history best remembered for mass terror and government-induced famines. "Dreary conventional stuff . . . trashy, melodramatic, false and inept" were opinions he tried to keep to himself for much of 1958, not only because it was unseemly to sully a competitor, but also because he knew Pasternak was going through hell in Moscow. The Soviet cultural authorities denounced him as a "pig" and worse.

In October 1958, Pasternak won the Nobel Prize for Literature, and *Doctor Zhivago* leapfrogged over *Lolita* to the number-one spot on best-seller lists all over the world. The Soviet Writers Union expelled Pasternak and forced him to decline the award. Nabokov, over time, became unhinged on this subject. Whether he saw himself as a more deserving Nobel candidate (probably), whether he resented sharing literary center stage with a fellow Russian whom he regarded as a lesser talent (possibly), or whether he simply thought *Zhivago* was a bad book (definitely), he began suggesting that *Zhivago*—far from being a courageous assertion of literary freedom in a prison society—was a piece of Soviet propaganda artfully transplanted to the West.

Both Nabokovs thought the explanation of how *Zhivago* surfaced in the West was too cute by half: "Any intelligent Russian would see . . . that the book is pro-Bolshevist and historically false, if only because it ignores the Liberal Revolution of spring, 1917," Vera wrote to her friend Elena Levin.[2] That is, the liberal revolution in which Nabokov's father played a historic role. QED, the book was a KGB plant.* Nabokov went so far as to suggest that Pasternak's mistress, Olga Ivinskaya, had written the manuscript. It's true that Ivinskaya, an accomplished editor and translator, had helped Pasternak translate some poetry. But she would have been generally unavailable to help with *Zhivago*, because in 1950 she began a five-year sentence in the gulag. Indeed, she miscarried Pasternak's child shortly after her arrest and imprisonment. Know them by the company they keep: It was Nabokov and the vestigial Stalinist stooges inside the USSR who pushed the ugly Ivinskaya theory. Nabokov likewise suspected that Alexander Solzhenitsyn was a KGB cat's-paw, until the USSR expelled him in 1974.[3]

Did Nabokov have a mean streak? Definitely, and it became more pronounced as he aged. Where did it come from? His first biographer, Andrew Field, who felt the razor's edge of Nabokov's scorn, thought Nabokov was deeply influenced by his literature teacher at the Tenishev school, the Symbolist poet and cynic V. V. Gippius. Gippius was the only schoolteacher whom Nabokov mentioned in his memoirs. Another Tenishev student, the famous poet Osip Mandelstam, recalled that Gippius taught "literary malice," "a literary posture," Field writes, "which to a certain extent [Nabokov] has never abandoned." "There is something

---

* More like a CIA plant, really. "We—the CIA—published the first Russian language version of Dr. Zhivago in the West," the Chavchavadzes' son David (a CIA officer) told his daughter Sasha for her family memoir, *Museum of Matches*. "We hoped that it would be read by as many people as possible in the Soviet Union and abroad. I gave Edmund Wilson his first copy of the book. I saw no reason not to."

bestial about the portrait of Gippius," the scholar Clarence Brown wrote in his biography of Mandelstam: "Paradoxically the love of literature was nurtured in his students by a man who hated literature, who saw in the length and breadth of its history an ample field for the spitefulness of his nature."

Nabokov eventually went to war with Field, contesting hundreds of biographical details, including this one: "The Tenishev school's inflicting Gippius upon me is no reason for your repeating the process," he wrote.[4]

By contrast, Wilson embraced *Zhivago* fervently. His lengthy, laudatory review in *The New Yorker*, "Dr. Life and his Guardian Angel," placed *Zhivago* solidly in the firmament of great works of literature. After some lengthy throat-clearing in which he berated *Zhivago*'s translators for multiple errors and misconceptions of the Russian language,* Wilson finally arrived at his point of departure. *Zhivago* "is one of the very great books of our time," he declared. "It is not really a book about Russia," he continued.

---

* Not for the last time, Wilson seized hold of the wrong end of the language stick, accusing others of failing to master Russian. After the death of *Zhivago*'s cotranslator, Max Hayward, Patricia Blake—his frequent collaborator, companion, and devotee—decided to set the record straight: American editors "translating" Hayward's English edition introduced several of the mistakes that Wilson complained about. Then she struck: "The worst howler [a favored Nabokovism] was committed by Wilson himself in his review," she wrote in the 1983 introduction to Hayward's *Writers in Russia*. Wilson botched the allusion *na tom svete* (in this world) and accused the translators of distorting Pasternak's cosmology, which Wilson had elevated into the Second Coming of the Christian Novel. Blake acidly and correctly accused Wilson of misunderstanding a "simple and straightforward" phrase that "would be clearly understood by a first-year Russian student."

But wait—she wasn't done. "So gross a mistake raised the question—later to be pursued with a vengeance by Vladimir Nabokov—of Wilson's proficiency in Russian. It would seem that this most erudite man's great weakness was that he loved to display linguistic expertise he scarcely possessed." But this story had a happy ending. The bibulous Hayward, who "went on a bender in Cambridge that landed him in the hospital" after reading Wilson's *New Yorker* putdown of his translation, later "cheerfully agreed to meet with Wilson over cocktails in Boston. They never discussed the *Doctor Zhivago* translation and soon became drinking buddies." Blake neglected to mention that Hayward acted, ineptly, as one of Wilson's Russian-language advisers in the ensuing *Onegin* brouhaha.

"Its main theme is death and resurrection . . . the author never departed from his Christian ideal of taking every individual seriously as a soul who must be respected." Wilson jauntily compared Pasternak with Pushkin, Gogol, Tolstoy, and James Joyce, and finished his piece with a peroration seldom seen in book reviews then or since:

> *Doctor Zhivago* will, I believe, come to stand as one of the great events in man's literary and moral history. Nobody could have written it in a totalitarian state and turned it loose on the world who did not have the courage of genius. May his guardian angel be with him! His book is a great act of faith and art and in the human spirit.

Wilson waxed full-tilt mystical on *Zhivago*, doubling down on his questionable premise that the novel was a profoundly Christian work, pregnant with religious symbolism, for example, "the five barless windows in the house in Siberia are the five wounds of Jesus." He went even further in *Encounter* magazine, alleging that "the more one studies *Doctor Zhivago*, the more one comes to realise that it is studded with symbols and significant puns, that there is something in it of *Finnegans Wake*, and something of the cabalistic *Zohar*, which discovers a whole system of hidden meanings in the text of the Hebrew Bible."[5]

Pasternak, who was born Jewish and attended Russian Orthodox services, just shrugged when he read Wilson's *Encounter* article. "Whoever has seen such symbols in *Doctor Zhivago*," the author wrote to Max Hayward, "has not read my novel."

Nabokov was well aware of Wilson's *Zhivago*-philia. Wilson complained to their mutual friend Roman Grynberg that Nabokov was "behaving rather badly about Pasternak. I have talked to him on the telephone three times lately about other matters and he did nothing but rave about how awful *Zhivago* was. He wants to be the only Russian novelist in existence. It amuses me to see *Zhivago* just behind *Lolita* on the best-seller list, and I am wondering whether Pasternak—as they say about horse-races—may not nose her out."[6]

Nabokov kept close watch on the horse race taking place in the bookstores, and with the novels still battling for primacy on the best-seller lists nine months after publication, he goosed Putnam to keep pace with the opposition. "The *Zhivago* gang is doing its best to prop up the sagging doctor," he wrote Putnam's chief, Walter Minton. "Should we not do something in regard to our nymphet?"[7]

Wilson occasionally mailed Nabokov rubber-band-powered butterflies that would flutter out of envelopes containing their correspondence. Around this time, he sent Nabokov a paper butterfly, with one wing labeled "Lolita" and the other, "Zhivago." One wonders how that gift was received in Ithaca.[8]

The *Zhivago* contretemps cast a chill over the Nabokov-Wilson relationship. The biographer Brian Boyd notes that Nabokov chose this moment to ask James Laughlin, his first American publisher and Wilson's friend, to delete Wilson's fulsome blurb from *The Real Life of Sebastian Knight*. Laughlin knew as well as anyone that *Knight* owed its few sales in 1941 to the cachet of Wilson's endorsement. Boyd writes that Nabokov likewise took umbrage at Wilson's "writing so ecstatically about *Doctor Zhivago* while dismissing *Lolita* before reading it to the end."

Nabokov wrote to Minton at Putnam to ensure that his new publisher wouldn't solicit blurbs from Wilson for any of his future books. "Personally, I am against all endorsements," Nabokov wrote from his perch atop the best-seller lists, "especially the ones that come from old friends. In this case, however, I am prompted to say what I say by my utter disgust with Edmund's symbolico-social criticism and phoney erudition in regard to Doctor *Zhivago*."*[9]

THEIR DISAGREEMENTS ABOUT *Zhivago* concerned not only literature but also politics, where the two men's differences were starting to become more pronounced.

Nabokov vociferously objected to any account of the Russian Revolution that failed to document what he called the post-1905 "social movements" and what American leftists and Soviet propagandists called "bourgeois liberalism" in czarist Russia. Russia had a parliament starting in 1905, and in the same year eliminated prior restraint of the press. (Lenin's newspaper *Pravda* became legally available in 1912.) As Nabokov saw it, Russian history was not an all-or-nothing proposition. He felt that historically underinformed Americans always assumed that Trotsky, Lenin & Co. were the only alternative to czarist rule, and that the mystical workings of the dialectic assured that only Nicholas II or the Bolsheviks could have ruled Russia after 1917. Of course he knew differently, because his father, and dozens of influential politicians like him, had tried to bring constitutional democracy to Russia. In addition he knew that Russia *had* a semifunctioning constitu-

---

* As we shall see, Nabokov liked to mock his enemies by inserting them as recognizable caricatures in his fiction. So we are not surprised that "Dr. Mertvago" surfaces in his 1969 novel, *Ada*. The root of Zhivago's name is *zhiv*, meaning "life" in Russian. "Myortvy," spelled with an *e*, pronounced "yo," in Russian, means "dead."

tional democracy for about a decade, before its violent overthrow by Soviet power in 1917.

Wilson viewed himself as an expert on this subject. After all, he had written the book *To the Finland Station*, which explained to literate Americans the inevitability of Leninist rule. He had visited the Soviet Union—admittedly for only a few months—but he often pointed out that Nabokov knew only the Russia of his remembered childhood, the Russia that hadn't existed for decades, at the very start of their friendship.

"I do not want to be personal," is how Nabokov began one of his most didactic political lectures directed at Wilson, a portion of which he reproduced in *Speak, Memory:*

> Your concept of pre-Soviet Russia, of her history and social development, came to you through a pro-Soviet prism. When later on . . . the pressure of inescapable facts dampened your enthusiasm and dried your sympathy, you somehow did not bother to check your preconceived notions in regard to old Russia while, on the other hand, the glamor of Lenin's reign retained for you the emotional iridescence which your optimism, idealism and youth had provided. What you now see as a change for the worse ("Stalinism") is a change for the better in knowledge on your part.

Let me spell that out for you, Nabokov suggested:

> Under the Tsars (despite the inept and barbarous character of their rule) a freedom-loving Russian had incomparably more possibility and means of expressing himself than at any time during Lenin's and Stalin's regime. He was protected by law.

There were fearless and independent judges in Russia . . . Periodicals of various tendencies and political parties of all possible kinds, legally or illegally, flourished and all parties were represented in the Dumas.[10]

Wilson wasn't going to let Lenin go just to please Nabokov. (Mary McCarthy once observed, "It was a mistake for Edmund to like Lenin, but that was the only way he could believe in the Russian Revolution.") In an essay published in 1949, Wilson wrote that Lenin "was fond of fiction, poetry and the theater, and by no means doctrinaire in his tastes," citing Lenin's wife as his source.[11] Nabokov thought this was perfect poppycock. "When Lenin says 'Pushkin,'" he wrote, "he is not thinking of our Pushkin, but of an average Russian mixture of a) school manuals, b) Tchaikovsky, c) hackneyed quotations, d) a kind of safe feeling about Pushkin as being 'simple and 'classical.'"

Entrusted with editing the Nabokov-Wilson correspondence, Simon Karlinsky sided with Nabokov in this argument. In his 1937 essay, "Marxism and Literature," Wilson wrote that the greatest literary writers of Russia's early twentieth century were Lenin, Trotsky, and the poet Alexander Blok, also a favorite of Nabokov's. "Wilson took almost no notice of the remarkable Silver Age of the early twentieth century," Karlinsky noted, citing the famous literary flowering that included Anton Chekhov, Leonid Andreyev, the Nobel Prizewinner Ivan Bunin, as well as the poets Sergei Esenin, Marina Tsvetayeva, and Vladimir Mayakovsky.[12]

Wilson's myopic and ideologically skewed vision of Russian literature was entirely of his own making. Ironically, it was the eccentric double émigré D. S. Mirsky, a Russian nobleman (full name: Dmitry Petrovich Svyatopolk-Mirsky) who first introduced Wilson to Pushkin's poetry in Russian, and to Russian literature in general. Mirsky fought with the White Army against the Bolsheviks, and eventually landed in Great Britain, where he wrote his masterpiece, *A History of Russian Literature: From Its Beginnings to 1900*, which Nabokov praised as the best book of its kind in English or Russian.

In England, Mirsky taught at the University of London and turned toward Marxism, joining the British Communist Party. He reemigrated to the USSR in 1932, with the help of a pardon obtained by the writer Maxim Gorky. When Mirsky took his farewells of his London friends, Virginia Woolf confided to her diary: "I thought as I watched his eyes brighten and fade—soon there'll be a bullet through your head."

She wasn't far off. Wilson spent a great deal of time with Mirsky in Moscow in 1935, and disguised his identity, not very adroitly, in his published journals. Both men knew that the aristocratic anti-Bolshevik–turned–Communist was under constant suspicion in Stalin's Russia. In 1937 the inevitable happened. The secret police arrested Mirsky as a British spy and sent him to the gulag, to the frozen wilds of Kolyma in the northeast corner of Siberia. He died in 1939.*

Russia again divided Wilson and Nabokov a decade later, as Nabokov started cheerleading for America in its Cold War struggle against Nikita Khrushchev's Soviet Union. As Wilson became more and more disenchanted with American politics, Nabokov—

---

* Mirsky's fate remained unknowable until after Stalin's death in 1953. In Nabokov's collected letters, there is a 1949 inquiry from the Knopf editor Robert Glauber, soliciting a blurb for a new edition of Mirsky's famous *History*. Nabokov answered: "Yes, I am a great admirer of Mirsky's work. In fact, I consider it to be by far the best history of Russian literature in any language including Russian. Unfortunately, I must deprive myself of the pleasure of writing a blurb for it, since the poor fellow is now in Russia and compliments from such an anti-Soviet writer as I am known to be might cause him considerable unpleasantness." Nabokov could not have known that Mirsky had been dead for ten years.

flush with *Lolita* earnings and living in Switzerland—became a flag-waving Yankee. (Did he think America could "win" the Cold War, topple Soviet power, and restore him to the childhood fairy-land of *Speak, Memory*? Perhaps.) Wilson had evolved into a ban-the-bomb-style enemy of the national security state, but Nabokov was all for bombs, the more the merrier. He would gladly have loaned the Strategic Air Command his maps of Moscow and St. Petersburg if he thought that would hasten the demise of what he had always viewed as the "evil empire."

Wilson began his career as a man of the Left, and by the mid-1950s he had become reenergized in his disdain for American capitalism. There is an early inkling of what later became an obsession in a 1955 letter to the Italian critic and scholar Mario Praz. Wilson half-jokingly claimed he might be "vaporized" because he had discovered that his Talcottville house in upstate New York sat next to a radar station, and that "there is a mysterious 'government project' not far away, enclosed in an iron fence. . . . In my opinion, the inhabitants of the United States ought to strike against paying the income tax till the government ceases to spend money on this insanity."[13]

Wilson developed some kooky political notions in the 1950s and 1960s, among them that 69 percent of the government's budget was devoted to military spending, which was not true. Notoriously, he had been pursuing his own tax boycott of the U.S. Treasury since 1941. For many years he didn't pay taxes because he preferred to spend his money on foreign travel, sumptuous meals, and private schools for his children. During the fat year of *Hecate's* best-sellerdom, he had plenty of cash, but continued to stiff the IRS. Wilson thought he "could always attend to this obligation later," and the one time he decided pay a tax bill—his 1955 book on the Dead Sea Scrolls sold well—his check bounced.

Even though he admitted in a moment of weakness that "my original delinquency was due not to principle but to negligence,"[14] Wilson started bruiting his antigovernment principles far and wide. In his 1962 introduction to *Patriotic Gore*, an overview of Civil War literature, Wilson plunged even more deeply into America-loathing. Comparing Abraham Lincoln to Lenin ("parallel imperialists") was provocative, but he didn't stop there. He again accused "the United States of Hiroshima" of spending 70 percent of its revenues on nuclear and bacteriological weapons. He added, decades before most Americans had ever heard of the National Security Agency: "We are, furthermore, like the Russians, being spied upon by an extensive secret police, whose salaries we are required to pay." Wilson's tax-related radicalism brought a knowing smile to friends' faces. "What are you going to say?" Jason Epstein asked, rhetorically. " 'I felt like cheating the government all those years?' You have to turn it into some kind of statement."

In his review of Wilson's 1963 philippic *The Cold War and the Income Tax*, Epstein alluded to a powerful character trait that ran in the Wilson family: cussedness. As mentioned, Wilson's father had refused to own stocks, considering them to be empty speculations. Wilson was never vaccinated; no one knows why. Certain things he did not do: He did not accept an honorary degree from Harvard, and he did not accept a life-extending pacemaker when his heart started to fail him. He did not pay his taxes, and it caused him no end of grief.

In his income tax jeremiad, Wilson concluded, "I have finally come to feel that this country, whether or not I continue to live in it, is no longer any place for me."

Nabokov, by contrast, loved the United States, especially since he savored the luxury of not living there, thus avoiding many of those taxes that were so bedeviling his old friend. Enriched beyond his wildest dream by the international sales of *Lolita*, he took the money and ran, eventually coming to rest in Montreux, Switzerland, on the shores of Lake Geneva. In January 1964, Edmund and Elena Wilson, returning their daughter Helen to school in Gstaad, traveled to Nabokov's digs at the Montreux Palace Hotel to spend a few evenings socializing.

Their famous correspondence and their frequent meetings had been in abeyance. This was Wilson's first trip to Europe since Nabokov had left the United States. Their disagreements over *Lolita* and *Doctor Zhivago* had dampened their earlier, ebullient exchanges.

"We found Volodya Nabokov living, as Elena said, like a prince of the old regime," Wilson wrote in his journal. "He was a more amiable and a more genial host than I had ever known him to be. The ready money had made all the difference. But they live as they have always lived, in modest enough rooms. He hunts butterflies in the summer and in the winter they see almost nobody. Volodya, but not Vera, has a certain nostalgia for the States."[15]

Nabokov's German publisher Heinrich Ledig-Rowohlt came to dinner, and Wilson sold him the German rights to *Hecate County* "on excellent terms." Rowohlt later marveled to Vera at the two men's "conversational fireworks . . . on the virtues of literature."[16] That was business as usual for Wilson and Nabokov, of course. "He and I disagree on everything in literature except Pushkin," Wilson told an interviewer not long before this, their final meeting.[17]

Pushkin would be the last to go.

5

Meet *Eugene Onegin*

It is almost impossible to explain to non-Russian speakers what *Eugene Onegin* is, and why Russians regard it as the unrivaled masterpiece of their literary canon. To educated Russians, *Onegin* is simply everything, as if all of Shakespeare's comedies and tragedies were supercollided into a narrative poem of five-thousand-plus lines, which many of them can quote at extraordinary length.

Onegin is everywhere, once you start to look. There is a famous passage from Eugenia Ginzburg's memoir, *Journey into the Whirlwind*, describing her interminable train trip to the gulag in 1937. As a diversion on the hellish journey, she recited poetry to her fellow inmates in the crowded railway car. A furious guard assumed she was reading from a concealed book, and to prove him wrong, she recited all of *Eugene Onegin* from memory. "As I went on reciting, I kept my eyes fixed on the two guards," Ginzburg wrote. "The Brigand at first wore a threatening expression: she'd get stuck in a minute, and then he'd show her! This gave place by degrees to astonishment, almost friendly curiosity, and finally ill-concealed delight."[1]

Perhaps you or I have read a half dozen of the Russian classics, such as Ivan Turgenev's *A Sportsman's Sketches*, or Leo Tolstoy's two epic novels, *War and Peace* and *Anna Karenin* (as Nabokov insisted on calling it*). Or Fyodor Dostoyevsky, for instance the marvelous, immersive *The Idiot*, or *The Devils*, a discursive, seemingly endless meditation on nineteenth-century progressive and revolutionary ideologies.

Then we pick up *Eugene Onegin: A Novel in Verse*, a slender volume of eight verse chapters, sometimes called cantos, in translation. There's not much to it. Some editions include a short canto called "Eugene's Journey," a rambling travelogue of czarist Russia, originally intended to be chapter 8, which Pushkin cut from the final poem. Thus the former chapter 9 became the current final chapter 8. Some editions include portions of a chapter 10, which reintroduces Eugene after the unresolved finale to the "real" chapter 8, and plunges him into post–Decembrist Uprising politics. (Several of Pushkin's friends participated in that half-baked revolt, aborted at birth in St. Petersburg's Senate Square in 1825.) Chapter 10's picaresque fate mirrored that of its storm-tossed author. Its opening lines about Czar Alexander I—"A ruler weak and wily / A baldish fop, a foe of toil"—guaranteed it would never see the light of day. Pushkin apparently burned the eighteen fragments of the chapter after committing them to memory. He recorded portions of it among his papers, albeit partly enciphered in a code that was decrypted only in 1910.

Further doubt attends the "final" or actual structure of the poem, because the perpetually broke, fast-living Pushkin com-

---

* It was Nabokov's contention that only Russian female performers like the ballerina Anna Pavlova merited feminization, with the added *a*, of their family names. This came off as a silly quirk, certainly to his wife Vera, who signed her letters "Véra Nabokova."

posed the chapters out of order, published each one separately for ready cash, and even mortgaged certain chapters to pay gambling debts.* Honoring a convention of Romantic poetry, Pushkin waxed endlessly about his "muse." But it was not some goddess in a diaphanous gown who wielded the greatest influence on the composition of *Onegin*, it was the czar's censor.† Most *Onegin* editions have blank swaths of text in place of the missing stanzas, either deleted by the censor or by the poet anticipating censorship, or, in some cases, by a playful Pushkin *pretending* to have been censored. Czar Nicholas I famously appointed himself to be Pushkin's censor, but in practice his chief of police Alexander von Benckendorff reviewed the poet's work. Any intimations of "freedom," even those wrapped in the most convoluted metaphors or euphemisms, were unlikely to appear in print.

Onegin is a peripatetic tale, transporting the reader from St. Petersburg to the gentryfolk's country estates, to Moscow and back to Petersburg. Thanks to censorship, that was the story of its creation. Pushkin composed most of *Onegin* while in exile, serving penance for verses championing the liberation of the serfs or some equally unpalatable idea.

Onegin does not sing in translation. The translations aren't as awful as Nabokov insisted they were, but they're not great, either. Translations, it has been said, are like one's mistress. She can be

---

* Chapter 2 famously "slid down [was lost] on an ace," a friend of Pushkin's reported. Pushkin replied: "I did not lose Chapter Two to you, what I did was pay you my debt with its published copies." Nabokov notes that "it is of psychological interest" that Pushkin cut two delightful stanzas about his passion for gambling from the final version of chapter 2. Separately, in 1826, Pushkin admitted to a friend, "Instead of writing Chapter Seven of *Onegin*, I go and lose Chapter Four at [cards]—which is not funny."

† "In Russia, the censorship department arose before literature; its fateful seniority has always been in evidence."—Vladimir Nabokov, *The Gift*

beautiful or she can be faithful, but she cannot be both. *Onegin* is the object lesson here.

It is also hard to explain what *Eugene Onegin* is about. Yes, it's the story of a few years in the life of the young dandy Onegin, a spoiled society rake who swans around St. Petersburg, sampling the finest things the "Paris of the North" has to offer. The famous first chapter reads like the old Neiman-Marcus catalog of luxury extravagances, bristling with what we could call product placements. More than once in the poem, Eugene checks his elegant, French-made Breguet watch, still advertised in the pages of *Vanity Fair* today. He looks in at Pierre Talon's fashionable restaurant

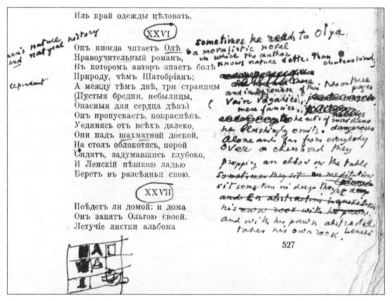

Page 527 of Nabokov's "bedside Pushkin," in which he sketches out a chess move mentioned in *Onegin* 4.27—the distracted, lovelorn Vladimir Lensky intends to move his pawn but takes his own rook instead. *(Princeton University Library)*

on the Nevsky Prospekt to drink some "comet" champagne, the famous vintage of 1811, when astronomers tracked the so-called Great Comet for almost nine months.

From chapter 1 Eugene repairs to the country estate he has inherited from his uncle, to launch into what passes for the novel's plot. He meets the beautiful Larin sisters, the dreamy, naive poet Lensky, and we move on from there. The characters are thinly drawn, ideal for the well-known Tchaikovsky opera ("The vile Tchaikovsky opera"—Nabokov) but too insubstantial to feature in the great European novels of the later nineteenth century. Tchaikovsky hits the high notes: the serf girls' lyrical madrigal; the lovestruck Tatiana's pleading letter to Eugene; the duel with Lensky, and the unsatisfying ending in which none of the main players lives happily ever after—least of all Lensky, whom Eugene killed in their duel.

Leaving aside the rickety plot, there arises the question of what and who shows up in Pushkin's "free novel." Pushkin includes himself as a character in the book, as well as many of his Petersburg friends and occasional celebrities. In one example of "reality"— the word Nabokov insisted could appear only between quotation marks—intruding into *Onegin*, Pushkin's friend Prince Peter Vyazemsky sits down next to Tatiana at a Moscow soiree and "begins to beguile her mind." The debauched Vyazemsky was notoriously bad company, and one of Pushkin's favorite sources of obscene epigrams. A clued-in reader would peruse 7.49, and think: Watch out, Tatiana!

Pushkin evinces admiration for Laurence Sterne's *Tristram Shandy* by wandering off into unprovoked, gorgeous digressions about ladies' feet, about the quality of winter frost, or the mating habits of provincial nobodies. *Onegin* revels in tricks we would today call postmodern. Pushkin dismissively includes his "Invocation to the Muse" at the end of chapter 7, writing:

> *That's all, and I am glad it's over,*
> *My debt to classicism paid:*
> *Though late, the Invocation's made.*

In chapter 5 he mocks his own digressions, specifically:

> *Dear girlish feet, it's time no more*
> *On your slim trail to court distraction:*
> *[And] keep this Chapter Five as free*
> *Of such digressions as may be.*

The twentieth-century writer and critic Andrei Sinyavsky accused Pushkin of "writing a novel about nothing." He couldn't abide the poem's digressive flights: "The author loses the thread of his narration, wanders off, marks time, beats around the bush and sits it out in the underbrush, the background of his own story."[2]

The critic Vissarion Belinsky ("the famous but talentless Vissarion Belinski," according to the unrelenting Nabokov[3]), who championed Pushkin to a later generation, memorably called *Onegin* "an encyclopedia of Russian life." But it is not. With the original "political" chapter 10—or was that 9?—expunged, there is zero political and precious little socioeconomic content or commentary in the novel at all. Nabokov gets this right: *Eugene Onegin* "is not 'a picture of Russian life,'" he wrote:

> It is at best the picture of a little group of Russians, in the second decade of the last century, crossed with all the more obvious characters of Western European romance and placed

in a stylized Russia, which would disintegrate at once if the French props were removed, and if the French impersonators of English and German writers stopped prompting the Russian-speaking heroes and heroines.[4]

How to explain the immortal allure of this impossible poem? Pushkin created his own metrical system, the "Onegin stanza," to tell Eugene's story, and it is strikingly beautiful in the original. The sonnets are unyielding in their iambic tetrameter rhythm, in their rhyme scheme—*ababccddeffegg*—and rigidly committed to a defined interplay of masculine and feminine rhymes—*fmfmffmmmfmmfmm*. (A masculine rhyme ends in one syllable; a feminine, or double rhyme, ends in two.) Here is the retired British diplomat Sir Charles Johnston precisely emulating the famous stanza in his 1977 translation:

> *Was this the Tanya he once scolded*
> *In that forsaken, distant place*
> *Where first our novel's plot unfolded?*
> *The one to whom, when face to face,*
> *In such a burst of moral fire,*
> *He'd lectured gravely on desire?*
> *The girl whose letter he still kept—*
> *In which a maiden heart had wept;*
> *Where all was shown . . . all unprotected?*
> *Was this that girl . . . or did he dream?*
> *That little girl whose warm esteem*
> *And humble lot he'd once rejected? . . .*
> *And could she now have been so bold,*
> *So unconcerned with him . . . so cold?*
> —*Onegin* 8.20

The verses have an astonishing levity in Russian, a language that can stack up heavily on the palate. It is almost impossible to resist the very bearable lightness of "this light name, Pushkin," as the poet Alexander Blok called him. (*Pukh* means "down" or "fluff" in Russian.) Sinyavsky elaborated that "Lightness in relation to life was the foundation of Pushkin's conception of the world, that feature of his character and biography. Lightness in verse became the condition of his creativity."[5]

Pushkin and *Onegin* are often likened to Byron, whose work Pushkin knew and admired. I think Pushkin more closely resembles Alexander Pope, for his predilection for mischief (though Byron certainly competes in that category) and for his "light" satirical tone that belies its serious intent. Pope "lisp'd in numbers" from an early age, and Pushkin likewise. At age sixteen "I started to speak in rhyme," he wrote in an early poem to one of his lyceum teachers. *Onegin* seems to be a very light product indeed.

"Eugene Onegin—like champagne / Its effervescence stirs my brain" is how the novelist Vikram Seth described the effect of reading the poem he reworked into *The Golden Gate*, a cascade of 690 gleaming *Onegin* stanzas that Gore Vidal called "the Great California Novel" when it was published in 1986.*

Onegin is some of the most beautiful Russian poetry ever written. Its organization is chaotic. It is all very Russian.

Being Russian, it is not only beautiful and raggedly assembled, it is also mysterious. It is Pushkinesque, thrown together rather like he lived his life, artfully and on the fly. Eugene in many ways resembled Pushkin, certainly the pre-exile boulevardier who roamed

---

* Seth never read a word of Pushkin in Russian. He repeatedly said that it was reading Johnston's meter-and-stress-faithful *Onegin* while killing time in a Palo Alto bookstore that inspired him to tackle *The Golden Gate*. The cognitive sciences professor Douglas Hofstadter, who translated *Onegin* in 1999, first discovered Pushkin by reading *The Golden Gate*.

Pushkin's own sketch of himself and Onegin, lounging on the Neva embankment. *(Courtesy of Wikimedia Commons)*

the Nevsky in his fashionable, dark "Bolivar" hat. The *Onegin* manuscripts teem with small illustrations, mostly portraits of Pushkin's friends and lovers, and the author even drew a famous sketch of himself and Eugene lounging on the Palace Embankment, across the Neva from the great symbol of czarist authority (and tyranny), the Peter and Paul Fortress.

It is impossible to avoid the feeling that Pushkin dwelled in his novel, and he was known to comment on its characters' behaviors in odd moments. "Do you know that my Tatiana has rejected Onegin?" he wrote to a friend. "I never expected it of her." Pushkin being Pushkin, he even wrote a vulgar epigram featuring a Tatiana "beset with stomach throes" (Nabokov's translation) who wipes her ass with a newspaper that had incurred the poet's wrath.

Most ominously, Pushkin replayed the minutiae of Eugene's fateful chapter 6 duel with Lensky in his own life, eleven years after writing the famous scene. Just as in the novel, a Paris-made

LePage pistol fired the fatal shot. Like Lensky, Pushkin perished for reasons that seem opaque at best; he called out a young French officer, Georges-Charles D'Anthès, who may or may not have been paying too much attention to the poet's young wife.* Just thirty-seven years old, Pushkin was widely acknowledged to be Russia's greatest poet. "The sun of our poetry has set!" read a short necrology in the *Russian Invalid* newspaper. "Every Russian heart knows the whole value of this irrevocable loss and every Russian heart will be lacerated." The czar's ministers saw the crowds swelling outside Pushkin's home, and quickly moved his funeral from St. Isaac's Cathedral to a small church. Fearing a political riot, the authorities insisted that Pushkin's funeral bier be transported to the church at night, and forbade university professors and students from attending the poet's last rites.

SOME OFT-TOLD STORIES are surely true. In 1949 Vladimir Nabokov had begun teaching his famous lecture course on Russian literature to undergraduates at Cornell University. When citing passages from Nikolai Gogol or Leo Tolstoy, Nabokov habitually translated excerpts from the text himself. Nabokov liked to rail against the established translators of nineteenth-century Russian masterpieces like Constance Garnett or David Magarshack, but he wasn't eager to supplant them. For one thing, it didn't pay. (Nabokov signed a contract to translate *Anna Karenina*—sorry, *Anna Karenin*—into English, but never delivered a manuscript.

---

* Nabokov spots another coincidence, if there can really be such a thing: Pushkin shoehorns his lover Zizi Wulf—he is making a joke about her un-wasp-like waist—into a banquet scene that takes place just two days before the fictional Lensky's death. The real Zizi dined with Pushkin in St. Petersburg the night before his fatal duel.

He did devote huge amounts of time and energy to translating his own pre-1940 works from Russian into English.) He especially bemoaned the lack of even a serviceable *Onegin* in English. One can imagine him becoming tiresome on this subject, prompting Vera to utter the fateful words: "Why don't you translate it yourself?"

Why not indeed? And so began a fourteen-year-long journey to produce what Nabokov occasionally called his greatest masterpiece, a book he felt sure would become a best-selling cornerstone of twentieth-century letters.

A few years into the *Onegin* project, during which he published three novels and another translation, while keeping up his teaching schedule through 1959, Nabokov developed an elaborate theory of how the poem should be rendered into English. *Onegin* could be best rendered in English as a "pony" or a "trot," meaning as a literal translation, he argued, because Pushkin's watchworks-precise meter and rhyme scheme could never read into the English language. But earlier, in 1944, when he and Wilson were scrambling to dream up publishing projects, Nabokov translated a few perfectly rendered, rhymed, and metered "Onegin stanzas" and sent them to his friend. Not surprisingly, Nabokov's handiwork shines:

> *I see the surf, the storm-rack flying . . .*
> *Oh, how I wanted to compete*
> *With the tumultuous breakers dying*
> *In adoration of her feet!*
> —*Onegin* 1.33

"The *Onegin* fragment is good," Wilson responded, hurrying on to other matters. Then Nabokov sent yet another translated fragment, and Wilson gently tried to push him off from this bootless venture.* "Don't you think shorter things are more in order?"[6] Wilson wrote back. He pointed out that *Onegin* had already been translated, "though badly enough," several times. But Nabokov had the bit between his teeth, and in 1948 pitched Wilson his book idea: "Why don't we write together a scholarly prose translation of *Evgenii Onegin* with copious notes?" There is no record of a response.†

Nabokov persevered. In a 1949 letter he talked about tossing off "a little book on *Onegin*" for the Oxford University Press, a "complete translation in prose with notes giving associations and other explanations for every line."[7] In just five years he had accomplished a great deal, and in 1955 published a provocative *Partisan Review* essay titled "Problems of Translation: *Onegin* in English." Here he trotted out most of the points he would repeat a decade later, word for word, in the contumacious and self-assured introduction to his *Onegin*.

---

* Nabokov composed these three stanzas as part of a submission to Doubleday, for a jointly written book on Russian literature, with his translations to be accompanied by Wilson's commentary. That project never saw the light of day, although the authors eventually choked out separate books to placate the publisher.

Nabokov later translated one more *Onegin*-style stanza into rhymed, iambic English—one he wrote himself. The final paragraph of his 1938 Russian novel, *The Gift*, scanned as a perfect *Onegin* verse. When Nabokov himself translated the novel in 1963, he rendered this passage, quite beautifully, into a rhymed, perfectly metered *Onegin* stanza in English.

† There is no reference in this exchange to Wilson's own attempt at translating *Onegin*, in a 1936 *New Republic* article, "In Honor of Pushkin." After noting that "the poetry of Pushkin is particularly difficult to translate," Wilson translated some famous stanzas about the coming of winter into serviceable English prose, albeit not serviceable enough for the Vladimir Nabokov who published his *Onegin* in 1964. Nabokov seems to have caught up with Wilson's English *Onegin* when the piece appeared in one of Wilson's many compendia, *The Triple Thinkers: Twelve Essays on Literary Subjects*, released in 1948. He credits Wilson as "the first to have adopted unrhymed iambics for rendering *EO*"—the very approach Nabokov eventually landed on. He then points out nineteen instances of mistranslation in Wilson's three slender paragraphs. Wilson's biographer Jeffrey Meyers noticed that Nabokov's treatment of Wilson's work hardened between his original 1964 edition and the revised 1975 book. In 1964 Wilson was guilty of "a few minor inexactitudes." By 1975 he had committed "a number of inaccuracies."

Nabokov working at his desk at Cornell. The folders of his *Onegin* draft loom in the foreground. *(Photograph by Maclean Dameron, Cornell University Photo Sciences Dept., Division of Rare and Manuscript Collections, Cornell University Library)*

"It is impossible to translate *Onegin* in rhyme," he wrote, but he did allow that a translation could try to preserve the iambic beat of the original, varying line lengths from iambic dimeter to iambic pentameter. "Readable" translations were rubbish: "A schoolboy's boner is less of a mockery in regard to the ancient masterpiece than its commercial poetization." Previous translators were idiots: "There are four English complete versions unfortunately available to college students." Nabokov demanded that *Onegin* be translated into "absolute literal sense, with no emasculation and no padding," and—nota bene—"with copious footnotes, footnotes reaching up like skyscrapers to the top of this or that page."

"When my *Onegin* is ready," he concluded, "it will either conform exactly to my vision or not appear at all."

That same year Nabokov published a two-stanza poem—two *Onegin* stanzas, mind you—in *The New Yorker,* titled "On Translating *Eugene Onegin.*" The opening lines are famous:

> *What is translation? On a platter*
> *A poet's pale and glaring head,*
> *A parrot's screech, a monkey's chatter,*
> *And profanation of the dead. . . .*
>
> *Elusive Pushkin! Persevering,*
> *I still pick up Tatiana's earring,*
> *Still travel with your sullen rake.*
> *I find another man's mistake,*
> *I analyze alliterations*
> *That grace your feasts and haunt the great*
> *Fourth stanza of your Canto Eight.*
> *This is my task—a poet's patience*
> *And scholiastic passion blent:*
> *Dove-dropping on your monument.*[8]

The project grew and grew. In early 1953 Nabokov spent two months researching in Harvard's Widener Library, and amassed three hundred pages of draft commentary. He predicted that the book would be six hundred pages long.[9]

By 1958, when he finished the draft he would submit for publication, his manuscript was 2,500 pages.[10] When yesteryear's futurist, *Future Shock* author Alvin Toffler, interviewed Nabokov at the Montreux Palace in 1964 for *Playboy,* Nabokov pointed to his *Onegin* work product "over there on that shelf." There they were: three sixteen-inch-long shoeboxes, containing about five thousand annotated index cards.

6

What Hath Nabokov Wrought?

The book's path to publication was not smooth. Thanks to *Lolita*, Nabokov was a literary rock star, and publishers proved eager to sign up (almost) anything that rolled off the tip of his pen. Doubleday liked Nabokov, and vice versa, but the idea of publishing the four-volume, reduced-font, 1,895-page monster makes the editor Jason Epstein laugh fifty-plus years after the fact. "That crazy translation of *Eugene Onegin*? God no!" Epstein says. "No one would buy that! It's the work of a madman. Nabokov said it couldn't be done, and it couldn't. It's an impossible book, you can't read it." Nabokov's colleagues at the Cornell University Press likewise wanted no part of this white elephant. Ultimately, it was Epstein who found a safe haven for *Onegin*, at the nonprofit Bollingen Foundation Press, headquartered in Washington, DC.

Bollingen and Nabokov's *Onegin* would prove a fine fit. The philanthropist Paul Mellon's wife Mary Conover Mellon created the Bollingen Foundation to memorialize the life's work of the psychologist Carl Gustav Jung. The first time Mary heard Jung speak, she remarked, "Though I don't know what he means, this has something very much to do with me." Bollingen was the name of the Swiss town where Jung had built a small house for himself, with his own hands. Mellon was a name synonymous with money. Paul's father, Andrew, had been secretary of the treasury for more than a decade, and Paul donated to the public, among other things, Washington's National Gallery of Art. Paul Mellon had spent a semester at St. John's College, the Great Books mecca in Annapolis, Maryland, and developed a lifelong interest in the classical tradition and the liberal arts.

Bollingen was sui generis, often soliciting book projects from writers they admired, rather than relying on formal proposals. The editors were arch-mandarins, and distinguished themselves over the years by publishing not only Jung, but also the Buddhist scholar D. T. Suzuki, a famous translation of the *I Ching*, and perhaps most notably, Joseph Campbell's books, including the bestselling *Hero with a Thousand Faces*. Campbell once remarked that "I don't know if anybody would ever have heard of me if it hadn't been for Bollingen."[1]

Wallace Brockway, one of Bollingen's top editors, was initially enthusiastic about landing Nabokov. He described the *Onegin* translation as "altogether admirable and we should lose no time in 'signing him up' as they say in the trade-book houses. Mr. Nabakov [*sic*], who is a crotchety enough fellow, offers his version in a rather fierce spirit, but—I would say—rightfully so."[2] Brockway changed his tune a few months later when he started leafing through the hundreds of pages of the "Commentary" that accompanied the translation: "I must say at once that it presents a central problem that may not be solved without some controversy," Brockway wrote:

> That is, it takes for granted a reader who is as familiar with
> French as with English. Mr. Nabokov has the point of view of

an old-fashioned Russian of the better classes, one, that is to say, who quite normally spoke French to his equals and Russian to his servants. . . .

The work is addressed not merely to the cultivated, but to those so cultivated that they can take an unkeyed reference in their stride. For example, speaking of the bowdlerized translation of Theocritus by one of Wordsworth's sons, he says that what Wordsworth did to the text is far more immoral than what Comas did to Lacon—he refers here, but without keying it, to a pederastic situation in Theocritus so overt that even the most modern translator-editor of the text, A.S.F. Gow, puts the Greek Text into Latin.*

Nabakov's [sic] divagations are as errant as Balzac's, quite as interesting, and often more amusing. Some of them verge on the irrelevant, because he is compulsively impatient of timidity. He goes overboard, but always in the spirit of a great critic.[3]

Editing Nabokov would not be Brockway's problem. That honor redounded to William McGuire, a seasoned editor with many of the Jung publications to his credit. He would be aided by Bart Winer, the second copy editor Bollingen threw at the project, whom Nabokov came to like and admire, citing him by name in the introduction. Notwithstanding Brockway's "animadversions"—a word that crops up often when Bollingen staffers talk about Onegin—the foundation signed a contract in March 1959. Nabokov promised to deliver five hundred thousand words on Onegin, with an elaborate "Commentary," which Bollingen planned to

---

* Brockway is referring to the exchange between Comatas and Lacon in Idyll V, lines 41ff.: "Comatas: 'When I was buggering you and you were feeling the pain, these she-goats were bleating as they were being penetrated by the he-goat.' Lacon: 'When the time comes for your death and burial, you hunched-over thing, may you not get buried any deeper than the depth of that penetration of yours.'"

publish in a multivolume edition priced at $18.50 ($150 today). The foundation noted that Nabokov's most recent work, the novel *Pale Fire*, had sold thirteen thousand copies in its first year. They decided to print five thousand copies of *Onegin*. Nabokov received no advance, but a straight 10 percent royalty on all copies sold.

Nabokov proved to be a crotchety collaborator indeed. He would insist that the made-up names "Stalin" (Josef Djugash-vili) and "Stendhal" (Marie-Henri Beyle) appear between quotation marks. His draft index was aleatory, with the same book whimsically alphabetized by author, or by part of the title. Three years into the project, after McGuire had approached two Soviet institutions, the Pushkin Museum and the Pushkin House, for minor favors, Nabokov interposed a *nyet!* "I am afraid I object very strongly to any checking of queries in Russia," he wrote to McGuire in March 1962,

> because of the squeamish uncontrollable distaste I have for the Soviet regime. My book has been written in exile and is a triumph of exile. [I] would not like to be obliged directly or indirectly to any Soviet governmental institution. . . . Please let us drop the entire question of contact with Soviet Russia. This letter may make the delight of some obscure scholiast circa 2062.

Nabokov's penny-pinching became the stuff of legend in the Bollingen corridors. About a year before publication he asked the foundation to publish his ninety-two-page-long appendix to *Onegin*, "Notes on Prosody," as a separate, advance offprint for scholars. He had gotten wind of a competing effort from a graduate student(!) and wanted to plant his flag first. The complaisant foundation published two hundred copies and mailed them to Russian studies experts in North America and Europe. In some business relating to this special edition, Nabokov sent Bollingen a ten-dollar invoice, for copying costs. "The former rings oddly," McGuire wrote to Winer in May 1963, "in light of the Foundation's having laid out well over $1,000 to oblige him with the offprint."

Near the end of the editing cycle, the Bollingen editors flagged some potential legal problems in Nabokov's merciless shredding of previous translators. On the advice of unnamed "libel lawyers"— the objection seems to have come from Bollingen's editor in chief, John Barrett—Winer suggested "weeding out a few epithets that will not be missed" from the text. There followed a list of fourteen suggested deletions, for example, "Penguin Books English para-phrase (omitting 'execrable')"; "In his eagerness to (omitting 'that Soviet toady')." In his memoir of his years at Bollingen, McGuire wrote that "some of Nabokov's epithets . . . might border on char-acter assassination."

Concerning the *Onegin* foreword, McGuire wrote to Nabokov suggesting "that the aspersions be diluted here, since your opin-ions are made amply clear in the commentary." Nabokov scrawled "No!" in the left margin of McGuire's letter, then added in the right margin: "Whatever aspersions appear in my foreword should not be diluted." By return mail he elaborated: "Why on earth should I spare the feelings of [translators] Babette [Deutsch], Dorothea [Radin], Oliver [Elton], and the gallant Henry S[palding]—or of their publishers?"

Nabokov, apparently unfamiliar with the niceties of copyright, further bridled at Bollingen's boilerplate note of "gratitude" to these translators' publishers, and to Edmund Wilson's publisher, for permission to quote from their works. "I also object to my being 'grateful for permission to quote' them and Edmund Wil-

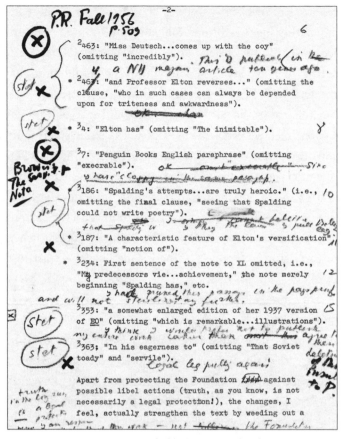

On an *Onegin* typescript, Nabokov insisting that his many
insults directed at rival translators remain—"stet"—in his text.
(Library of Congress, Bollingen Collection)

son. Why can't I quote if I like? It sounds awfully mawkish. To
whom am I 'grateful'? 'Grateful' is a big word." In the end Bollingen merely "acknowledged permission for the use" of quotes from
the earlier translators and Wilson, all of whom Nabokov disparaged in his "Commentary."

Two months later Nabokov was still tangling with Bollingen, asserting his right to heap mud upon whomever he liked. "I would like those lawyers of theirs to give me a single instance when a literary critic's describing a translator's mistake as 'ridiculous' or 'atrocious' or 'nonsensical' ever led to legal action on the part of that translator or publisher, or of their associated shades."

Bollingen eventually sought a legal opinion from the libel specialist Rene Wormser. He thought the chances of a defamation claim were "very slight." Wormser wrote that Nabokov could characterize the previous translations as "inaccurate and faulty" as long as he stopped short "of characterizing the previous translators as *intrinsically incompetent*. The factor of malice is important, and, in sum total, we see ridicule but not malice."[4]

In the end Nabokov made three of the requested fourteen deletions, and kept some lovely invective for his *Onegin* "Commentary." The Pushkin scholar N. L. Brodsky remained "that Soviet toady, in his servile eagerness," and Oliver Elton could "always be relied upon for triteness and awkwardness."

The Bollingen editors spooked easily, and Nabokov seemed to enjoy tormenting them. In October 1962, he advised, ominously: "It so happens that I have some free time this fall. . . . I intend to project myself into the Index." He then explained: "An index to a work like this should reflect its virtues and its shortcomings, its tone and personality (as I have proved in *Pale Fire*). It should be an afterglow and not a yawn."

The *Pale Fire* index, a characteristically Nabokovian mashup of erudition, brilliance, and obscurantism ("*Urban the Last*, emperor of Zembla, an incredibly brilliant, luxurious, and cruel monarch whose whistling whip made Zembla spin like a rainbow top"), was well known to Bollingen. McGuire divined the emanations of a "trick index" from Montreux, and hoped to snuff them out quickly. "If, as you fear, Nabokov has a trick index in mind for *EO*," Winer wrote to McGuire, "I think he should be discouraged at the very start. *EO* is not a novel, but a work of scholarship, and VN is not entitled to having a joke on those who buy the work, not to say on Bollingen."

McGuire dispatched Winer to Switzerland to talk Nabokov out of his funky indexing fantasy. Nabokov proved receptive to one-on-one handholding, and decided not to "project himself" into the index.

Bollingen's seven-year-long forced march shepherding *Onegin* into print, complete with coddling its demanding celebrity author, might have been more than they bargained for. But they wouldn't have begrudged the massive investment of editors' time, and huge printing costs, for their elegant edition. As Nabokov's friend Morris Bishop, the literature professor who recruited him to Cornell, sardonically observed: "Bollingen loves to lose money."[5]

Nabokov showed Alvin Toffler the *Onegin* raw materials in January 1964. The finished volumes were supposed to appear in April, when Bollingen hosted a reception for the Nabokovs in New York. Paul Mellon did not attend; *The New Yorker's* William Maxwell and Saul Steinberg, an artist whom Nabokov admired, did attend. Hugh Hefner was on the guest list—Nabokov read *Playboy* and would become a contributor—but it's unclear if he showed up. Edmund and Elena Wilson were invited, but they were traveling in Italy and Hungary at the time.

The Nabokovs' monthlong visit was the last trip the couple made to America. Nabokov read from his work at the 92nd Street Y in Manhattan, and at the Sanders Theatre at Harvard. He plugged *Pale Fire* but never mentioned *Onegin,* which wouldn't go on sale until June.

Mirabile dictu, the book appeared, six years after completion, all four volumes and 1,895 pages of it. What had Nabokov wrought? A doorstop composed of unequal parts hubris, genius, philological research carried to proctological extremes, heedless and needless provocation, often but not always informed by an exquisite literary sensibility. The translation itself took up only 257 pages. The amazing, relentless "Commentary" stretched into two volumes, covering 930 pages. Prefatory materials totaled 88 pages, and the index 107 pages. The Bollingen edition had two appendixes, the 92-page "Notes on Prosody," and a 60-page biography of Avram Gannibal,* the African hostage-turned-czarist-general who was Pushkin's great-grandfather. When Princeton University Press republished Nabokov's *Onegin* in 1975, they dropped the appendixes.

A photocopy of the 1837 edition of *Eugene Onegin,* printed in unreadably tiny Cyrillic type, occupied the final 310 pages of volume 4.

I don't like Nabokov's translation, which has provoked a panoply of reactions from adoration to horror. I would not go so far as Douglas Hofstadter to condemn "the implacably Nazistic Nabokov" for his "catastrophic" rendering of *Onegin,*[6] but it simply does not speak to me.† Having said that, I'll rescue a well-worn

---

* Russian hardens English *h*'s to *g*'s, with occasionally comical results, for example, Gumbert Gumbert and Gubert Gumphrey.

† Judge not lest ye be judged: Hofstadter developed an *Onegin* fixation, and devoted two years to creating his 1999 translation, unburdened by a deep knowledge of Russian. The translator Richard Lourie had a bit too much fun fricasseeing Hofstadter in *The New York Times:* "Hofstadter is much given to theories of translation, which to my mind resemble culinary theories of pudding—we all know where the real proof lies. He is constantly dodging the shadow of Nabokov." Lourie exposed a few of Hof-

Pushkinism from my tenth-grade memory: Nabokov's is a translation "to which one cannot remain indifferent."

Edmund Wilson will be carpet-bombing this translation soon enough. For now here are some examples of Nabokov's hyperliteralism placed at the nominal service of his hero Pushkin. Throughout, Nabokov cultivates an odd and off-putting vocabulary, which he generally defends on the grounds of accuracy. But why are Eugene's nail scissors "curvate" and not "curved"? Why does "the tomcat . . . wash his muzzlet with his paw"? What kind of word is "rememorate," which Nabokov uses as a synonym for "remember"? Why is *nega*, a very common word in *Onegin* and arguably even embedded in Evgeny's surname, which means "comfort" or "bliss," translated as "mollitude"? What is "ancientry"? What are "shandrydans"? What are "agrestic views"? I'll stop there.

Or not. How can Tatiana's plaint to her old nurse, "*Mnye skuchno*," possibly be translated "I am dull," when it translates

---

stadter's ghastly boners, for example, "In matters of the heart still virgin/With hope the lad began to burgeon," and tossed the "tortured syntax, groan-inducing rhymes and a language unlike that ever spoken by anyone on earth" onto the rubbish heap of literature. "It is flat, your translation," Lourie concluded, paraphrasing Flaubert to Turgenev on the subject of Pushkin.

Beware the cyberneticist-turned-translator! Here is part of Hofstadter's reply to Lourie, published a few weeks later in the *Times*:

I write to counter Richard Lourie,
Who tried to trash my Pushkin verse,
'Eugene Onegin.' In his fury,
He called it 'flat,' and even worse,
He claimed my English was deficient,
My Russian weak and insufficient—
I have to question why a critic
Would crudely crow, 'There's not a line
That sings or zings,' yet quote but nine
From o'er five thousand. Such acidic
But feckless words to flout my rhymes
Did not well serve The New York Times.

This is an Onegin stanza . . . of course.

very simply to "I am bored"?* Nabokov insists that *derevnya* always means "county seat," but it also means "village," and so on. He mocks four translators† for writing that the season's first snow fell in 5.1 "on the night of the third," but as a literalist he could surely appreciate that *na tret'ye v noch'* actually does means "on the night of the third." He may be right that Pushkin meant "on January second, after midnight," or not.

Nabokov had to maneuver *Onegin* through several editors at the Bollingen Foundation, which published the first edition in 1964. None of the editors could match Nabokov's Russian erudition, but they were excellent stylists who generally tried to save their wayward charge from himself. Ruth Mathewson, for instance, tried to steer Nabokov clear of "pal," a word that feels wrong standing in for the Russian *priyatel'*, or "friend." "Pal" is "a class word," Mathewson informed Nabokov, "identifying the speaker as a bum, a slob, a barroom hanger-on; or on a more sentimental and slightly more conscious level, a hick or a Rotarian."

"Pal" remained, although Mathewson did not; Bollingen shunted her aside in favor of Winer. In Nabokov's edition "pal" dis-graces the novel's famous envoi, where Pushkin bids the reader farewell: "Whoever you be, O my reader/Friend, foe—I wish with you/To part at present as a pal."

Ugh. It fell to Winer, who worked tirelessly on the *Onegin* manuscript, to point out that words such as "philologism," "indignated," and "stylopygian" occurred in neither the *Oxford English Dictionary* nor *Webster's International Dictionary*. "Philolo-

---

* In his "Commentary," Nabokov writes that "I am ennuied" was his second choice.

† Whomping on other translators, as we have seen, was a favorite Nabokov pastime. When he and his son, Dmitri, translated Mikhail Lermontov's *A Hero of Our Time* for Doubleday in 1958, Nabokov insisted that "this is the first English translation of Lermontov's novel." In a footnote he listed five English versions "known to me—all bad."

gism" stayed; "good little word," Nabokov scrawled on his galley sheet. The others vanished.

Ghastly syntax abounds. I opened Nabokov's *Onegin* at random to chapter 5, stanza 33, which begins: "Tragiconervous scenes/The fainting fits of maidens, tears/Long since Eugene could not abide."

Even Brian Boyd, who mounted an informed and assertive defense of Nabokov's translation in his two-volume biography, bridled at the writer's "frequent wrenchings of English word order." A case in point, from chapter 8, stanza 28:

> *Of a constricting rank*
> *The ways how fast she has adopted! . . .*
>
> *About him in the gloom of night,*
> *as long as Morpheus had not flown down,*
> *time was, she virginally brooded.*

"When a great stylist produces such ungainly English," Boyd wrote, "he has evidently decided on awkwardness for awkwardness' sake."

But the translation isn't what occupied Nabokov's eight years of intermittent drudge work in Harvard's Widener and Houghton Libraries, and in the New York Public Library. The 930-page "Commentary" enveloped the four volumes like a thick, dense smoke, although for a work supposedly aimed at the general public it's far from clear who could possibly get through it. The "Commentary" has its own brief foreword, repeating verbatim some of Nabokov's earlier 1955 animus toward previous translators ("The four 'English,' 'metrical' 'translations' . . . unfortunately available to students . . ."). Now in 1964 he piped a new member into their Hall of Shame: "Walter Arndt's . . . paraphrase, in burlesque English, with preposterous mistranslation."*

One stands in awe before the seemingly endless notes, which admix genius and madness in uneven proportions. There seems to have been no proverbial stone unturned, each one triggering a tiny, predictable landslide that one would have wished, in retrospect, to have avoided. There is score-settling right and left. Who could possibly imagine, or care, that a 1928 commentator misidentified the make of the pistol that killed our favorite author? (It's "LePage," not "Lgiage," Nabokov pedantifies.) Who is surprised that Stalin-era commentators, such as "the incredible Brodksi . . . who spells the title of Rousseau's work *Le Contrat Sociale . . .*" (*Contrat* is masculine, thus *Social* takes no *e*) see dialectical materialism under every couplet? Who expected anything less?

As early as the notes for chapter 1, Nabokov makes an unbrief detour to assure us that the "boredom of reading through the English, German, Polish, etc., 'translations' of our poem was much too great even to be contemplated." Then he quotes liberally from three substandard (by his lights) German *Onegins*, and from two Polish ones. "These violet and corn-poppy extracts"—he means the Polish ones—"are superior in circus value" to the German ones, he informs us.

But really, Vladimir. We thought we were buying an English

---

* Nabokov's copyeditor Winer confided to McGuire that "the Arndt condemnation seems mere pique, at someone who beat him to the gun, especially when others award Arndt a prize." (Inconveniently for Nabokov, Arndt's *Onegin* won the Bollingen Prize for Translation.) Literally days before the massive *Onegin* project went to press, Nabokov tried to shoehorn some anti-Arndt bile into the text. In an anti-translators screed embedded in a note to canto 8.17–18, Nabokov intended to describe Arndt's work as "this singularly unnecessary production in doggerel verse, full of omissions, additions, distortions and hilarious blunders." This squib did not make the cut.

translation of a Russian masterpiece. Understandably, perhaps a little French might wander in. But German? Polish? To which he responds: You ain't seen nothing yet. How about a page and a half on the lingonberry, disambiguated from the bilberry, the cowberry, the windberry, the German *Preiselbeere*, Thoreau's mountain cranberry, from Linnaeus's *Vaccinium myrtillus* and twenty other kinds of berries? "I expect some acknowledgement for all this information from future translators of Russian classics," Nabokov writes.

Some of this is charming, in its lucky-we-have-hours-to-burn-on-this-kind-of-thing way. Nabokov devotes at least a hundred pages of commentary to lines that Pushkin never published—variants, drafts, and stanzas either cut by the censor or cut by Pushkin in anticipation of official displeasure. A part of me admires Nabokov for translating Tatiana's famous letter to Eugene (3.31) into French, the language in which it was (fictionally) written. But Pushkin chose to publish the letter in Russian, in what he called his "weak translation" of the seventy-nine gorgeous lines. Nabokov offers us the hypothetical French version alluded to but ignored by Pushkin. Why?

Better: Why not?

A favorite moment, although it is a long moment indeed: The "Pedal Digression," Nabokov's name for forty lines of *Onegin*, starting at 1:30:8—

> *I like their little feet . . .*
> *Ah me, I long could not forget*
> *two little feet! . . .*
> *I still remember them, and in my sleep*
> *They disturb my heart.*

and ending with the famous image at 1:33—

> *I recollect the sea before a tempest:*
> *how I envied the waves*
> *running in turbulent succession*
> *with love to lie down at her feet.*
> *How much I longed then with the waves*
> *to touch the dear feet with my lips!*

What takes Pushkin 140 iambs to express takes Nabokov fifteen pages of dense analysis. The "Pedal Digression," Nabokov writes, "is one of the wonders of the work." "Neither Ovid, nor Brantôme, nor Casanova has put much grace or originality into his favorable comment on women's feet."

Nabokov quickly dismissed the banal suggestion that Pushkin may have been a foot fetishist (or ankle? or calf?):* "The passion for a pretty instep that Pushkin shared with Goethe would have been called 'foot-fetishism' by a modern student of the psychol-

---

* The translator/cyberneticist Hofstadter correctly notes that the Russian word *noga* and its diminutive *nozhky* "is a notorious Russian word that means both 'foot' and 'leg,' . . . therefore, in his sensual paean to sleek pairs of feminine appendages, Pushkin is referring just as plausibly to *legs* as to *feet*. . . . I present Pushkin as a 'leg man' rather than a foot fetishist." Hofstadter says a friend has labeled this obsession an "iambic diversion," a clever play on—never mind.

Hofstadter is probably wrong about Pushkin being a "leg man." Witness the testimony of the nineteen-year-old beauty Anna Kern, one of the poet's great loves: "Among the poet's singularities was that of having a passion for small feet, which in one of his poems he confessed to preferring to beauty itself."

But he is right that one Russian word means both "foot" and "leg." In a lengthy 2014 essay on translating *Anna Karenina* (surely 'Karenin'?), Masha Gessen makes this same point about *ruka*, the Russian word for "arm" or "hand." She parts company with translators Constance Garnett, Rosamund Bartlett, and others, when rendering the famous scene in which Anna's lover, Vronsky, finds her hand repellent. "I happen to think Tolstoy is writing about the arm," Gessen writes, "one of those two full arms that were so beguilingly set off by the black gown Anna wore to the ball in Part 1, Chapter 22, when she and Vronsky fell in love."

ogy of sex," a remark he doesn't bother to dignify with further explanation.* To hell with "the Viennese quack" and his epigones, and while we are at it, to hell with those idiot translators he's been telling us about. This stretch of the "Commentary" is particularly brutal on "bluff Spalding," "Solecistic Prof. Elton," and "Helpless Miss Radin" and includes what we would call today an unprovoked drive-by on Henri Troyat's 1946 Pushkin biography ("tritely written and teeming with errors"), which I recall reading with immense pleasure on a beach, as it happens (albeit a very cold beach), outside Riga, with waves licking at my feet. But I digress.†

The heart of Nabokov's divagation, however, is a whodunit: Whose footprints are these, he asks, flitting so gracefully across *Onegin*'s pages? "The search for a historically real lady, whose foot the glass shoe‡ of this stanza [33] would fit, has taxed the ingeniousness or revealed the simplicity of numerous Pushkinists," he writes.

---

* Another well-known man of letters shared Goethe and Pushkin's appreciation of the well-turned ankle: Edmund Wilson. "Like Alexander Pushkin, the Russian poet whom he so admired, he was susceptible to the charms of women's feet," Wilson's son, Reuel, recalled in his 1972 memoir. Reuel's half-sister, Rosalind, noted in *her* memoir that their father himself had small feet, and that upon meeting his soon-to-be-fourth wife Elena Mumm Thornton, he noticed that "she had prettier hands and feet than Mary McCarthy." "Kissing Elena's feet," Wilson wrote in his journal, "was erotically stimulating to me, and I would put my hand around her foot under the instep and squeeze it with an erotic pulsation."

Reviewing Wilson's journal collection *The Thirties* for *The New York Review of Books*, Gore Vidal counted twenty-four references to women's feet. Alluding to Wilson's "podophilia," Vidal wrote, "he could have made a fortune in woman's footwear."

† Why not digress? Nabokov's not-very-appealing habit of rubbishing his competitors and fellow writers also extended to his butterfly writing, to wit these examples from *Nabokov's Butterflies*, a beautiful collection of lepidoptery, edited by Brian Boyd and Robert Michael Pyle: Ben Leighton's "incredibly naïve paper"; William Holland's "Blunderfly Book"; Embrik Strand's "farcical nomenclatorial methods," and so on.

‡ There is a famous passage in Nabokov's 1957 novel *Pnin* in which the pusillanimous professor, whom it is hard not to equate with Mr. N. himself, explains that there never was a glass slipper, "that Cendrillon's shoes were not made of glass but of Russian squirrel fur—*vair*, in French." A *verre*-y understandable and amusing confusion, to be sure.

It is an interesting question because Pushkin had many, many lady friends, at least two of whom left memoirs of gamboling with the mutton-chopped young poet-exile at the seashore. The prime suspect is the beautiful Maria Rayevskaya, one of four children of Gen. Nikolai Rayevsky, a hero of the Napoleonic Wars. Pushkin knew the family intimately, and of course admired the general's attractive young daughters. Maria left a memoir ("remarkably banal and naïve"—Nabokov) in which she recalled playing in the waves with Pushkin at Taganrog, on the shore of the Azov Sea. The poet had hitched a ride south with the Rayevskys on his way to the Caucasus.

Maria recalled that Pushkin wrote "some charming verses" about the seaside idyll. Nabokov distrusts her memory because she gets her own age wrong. He proceeds to investigate Maria's older sister Ekaterina ("splendid-looking, goddess-like and proud") as the Lady of the Sea. In 1820 Pushkin spent three weeks in the Crimean village of Gurzuf, where Ekaterina and her mother were living in a rented seaside palazzo. Nabokov thinks Pushkin alluded to his infatuation with Ekaterina in some lines from "Onegin's Journey," the abandoned chapter 7 of an early draft. "The glass shoe does not fit [Maria Rayevski's] foot," Nabokov concluded after several pages of textual scholarship. "It may fit Ekaterina's, but that is a mere guess based on our knowledge of Pushkin's infatuation with her."

Nabokov dismisses with a hand wave a Soviet-era seminar ("heroically meeting amidst the gloom and famine of Lenin's reign") that suggests that Pushkin may have dallied in the surf with the Rayevsky girls' chaperone, or *dame de compagnie*. Then he advances his strongest candidate, Countess Elizaveta Vorontsova, the wife of the man overseeing Pushkin's exile in Odessa. Vorontsova was the lover of Alexander Rayevsky, one of

Pushkin's closest friends and the brother of the gorgeous sisters. This Alexander didn't mind Alexander Pushkin spending time with his mistress, because their relationship threw her husband, the governor-general of the southern province Novorossiya, off the scent. There is an 1834 letter from Pushkin's friend and confidante, Princess Vera Vyazemskaya, to her husband describing some tripartite Odessa wave dodging with Pushkin and Elizaveta Vorontsova. Later that year Pushkin sent Vera "the stanza I owe you," which Nabokov strongly suspects to be the famous and beloved verse 33 of chapter 1.

Whose feet are these?/He thinks he knows: "If the pair of feet chanted in XXXIII does belong to any particular person, one foot should be assigned to Ekaterina Raevski and the other to Elizaveta Vorontsov," Nabokov solomonically concludes. Then, after fifteen dense pages of occasionally lyrical scholarship, he says he hates "prototyping," or matching up real people and real events to characters and events in fiction. "I object to the prototypical quest as blurring the authentic, always atypical methods of genius,"[7] he wrote, adding later that "I am very much against stressing the human-interest angle in the discussion of literary works."

The entire "Pedal Digression," he concluded, is "of no interest whatsoever."

7

"He Is a Very Old Friend of Mine"

The Vladimir Nabokov vs. Walter Arndt contretemps was a bit like the shelling of Fort Sumter, a seemingly faraway and isolated incident that, when viewed in hindsight, signaled the beginning of a protracted war.

In March 1957, Arndt, a forty-year-old professor of Russian literature at the University of North Carolina, sent a letter to Nabokov in Montreux. The German-born Arndt had much in common with Nabokov. He attended Oxford and, like the Russian émigré, had weathered the midcentury Central European storms. Arndt abandoned his graduate studies in Slavic languages and literature in Warsaw and renounced his German citizenship to fight with the Polish army against the invading Germans in 1939. He was captured, escaped, and made his way to Istanbul, where he worked for the Office of Strategic Services, the precursor to the CIA. In the 1950s he changed careers and earned his doctorate in comparative linguistics and classics from the University of North Carolina, where he taught classics until moving to Dartmouth in 1966.

Arndt was spending a sabbatical year at Harvard, and had started work on a translation of *Eugene Onegin*. He didn't know that Nabokov was close to finishing his mammoth translation-

and-annotation project. He remembered noticing, in *The Russian Review*, the three *Onegin* stanzas translated by Nabokov, and sent along twelve sample stanzas of his own translation, soliciting "outside judgment, encouragement, or authoritative condemnation."

There is no record of a reply.

Two years later Arndt posted a second letter, this time on UNC stationery. He was planning to publish his *Onegin* translation, which he enclosed for the master's perusal. Arndt now understood that Nabokov was working on his own translation, and he asked about specific publication plans. For obvious reasons Arndt's publisher, Dutton, hoped to avoid direct competition between the two books.

Less than a week later Vera Nabokova, who handled much of her husband's correspondence, responded. "You need not be concerned about my husband's *Eugene Onegin* book," she wrote. "It will have actually nothing* in common with yours. . . . He finds your translation full of blunders, the reason for this being your insufficient knowledge of the Russian language as well as of the literary and historic background of the novel." More scorn followed. (Her asterisk pointed to this footnote: "Except the word "lingenberry"[*sic*] which you borrowed from him."[1])

In 1963, amid a blizzard of correspondence passing between New York City and Switzerland, the Bollingen Foundation sent Nabokov a clipping of an ad for Arndt's *Onegin*, asking if he would like to see it. "Yes, I would like to see the 'brilliant' translation of Walter Arndt—whoever that is," Nabokov answered, and this time he paid very close attention indeed. A few months later he published a devastating takedown of Arndt's *Onegin* in *The New York Review of Books*.

At the beginning Nabokov needed to say why he was attacking a rival translation so close to his own publication date, just a few

months in the future. He had resolved to "master my embarrass-
ment" and perform a public service, he explained: "Something
must be done, some lone, hoarse voice must be raised, to defend
both the helpless dead poet and the credulous college student from
the kind of pitiless and irresponsible paraphrast whose product I
am about to discuss."

There follow several thousand words of vintage Nabokovia:
the airy dismissal of Arndt's years of work ("twisting some five
thousand Russian iambic tetrameters [into] similarly rhymed
English . . . is a monstrous undertaking"); the vitriol ("sustained
stretches of lulling poetastry and specious sense"); the condescen-
sion ("anything too far removed from [Hi-how-are-you-I'm-fine]
becomes a pitfall"); the inevitable dyageddit? pun ("the meager
fare . . . becomes a Gargarndtuan feast"); the unintended malapropism ("which, as boners go, is a kind of multiple fracture");
and, of course, boyish one-upmanship, the homage that pedantry
pays to erudition. Nabokov scores Arndt for misidentifying "racemose bird cherry" as "alder," but notes that "the harmful drudges
who compile Russian-English dictionaries have at least, under
cheryomuha, 'black alder,' i.e. 'alder buckthorn,' which is wrong,
but not as wrong as Arndt's tree."*

Nabokov conveniently ignored Arndt's gracious acknowledgment of his aid in the preface ("Several emendations were suggested by Vladimir Nabokov's criticism," apparently referring
to Vera's scathing letter), but he could not ignore the fact that

---

* Nabokov blissfully ignored the near-impossibility of scanning "racemose bird
cherry" into iambic tetrameter, but never mind that. How did *he* translate *cheryomuha* in *his Onegin*? Nabokov devoted several pages of his "Commentary" to this
(un)thorny question, again reviling the "harmful drudges," the dictionarists, and
even eschewing the "usually reliable [four volume, Vladimir] Dahl's dictionary,"
which calls the tree mahaleb. [Nabokov instead appealed to the most trusted lexico-
logical source of all: himself. "I now formally introduce the simple and euphonious
'racemosa,' used as a noun and rhyming with 'mimosa.'"

Arndt's smooth, rhyming translation had won the Bollingen Poetry Translation Prize. Bollingen as in the same foundation that was underwriting his *Onegin*. A richly undeserved reward, Nabokov assured his *New York Review* readers. He named the selection committee of Harvard and Yale professors, then added: "One cannot help wondering if any of the professors really read this readable work"—"readable" being a Nabokovian insult, akin to "workmanlike"—"or the infinitely great poem of their laureate's victim."*

The Fort Sumter–ish rule governing these low-stakes literary skirmishes is: Always return fire. Thus ensued one of those prissy, overdetermined exchanges that seem the special province of the *New York Review*.

Arndt professed to be unsurprised by Nabokov's outburst: "All prior invaders of the precinct of *Onegin* translation have found him coiled at the exit (see his article in Partisan Review, Fall, 1955) and have been dosed, jointly and severally, alive or posthumously, with much the same mixture of arrogance, cuteness, and occasional distortion."

One would wish to say that Arndt, a facile writer, a top-drawer scholar, and a clever fellow, gave as good as he got, but that was not the case. Still, if he didn't show up at this knife fight with a LePage pistol, he hadn't come unarmed either. Arndt pointed out that Nabokov cut plenty of corners when he tried to Anglicize the *Onegin* stanza in *The Russian Review;* it comes with the territory. Arndt displayed the kind of *haut-en-bas* didacticism so favored by *New York Review* polemicists when he suggested that

---

* Ivy League jurors were a novelty. The Library of Congress had awarded the prize until 1948, when it was bestowed on Ezra Pound, who had suffered a mental breakdown after being indicted for treason during World War II. The government exited the laurels-on-Parnassus business double-quick and handed it over to Bollingen.

Nabokov, "while not perhaps trained in linguistics or phonometrics," should know that English words like "power" and "fire" can scan as one, two, or one-and-a-half syllable words, depending on usage, especially in poetry.

Arndt argued that Nabokov, "with the brand of fairness peculiar to him," was having entirely too much fun at his expense. He was right. He countered the master's nastiness with a tempered promise: "The therapeutic portions of Mr. N.'s fervid physic will also be gratefully embodied, with acknowledgment, in any second edition."

They were. In subsequent editions Arndt graciously acknowledged Nabokov's "prodigious two-volume commentary—probably his most enduring, certainly his most endearing, opus." Arndt wrote that his own work "was superabundantly complemented by the boundless learning of Mr. Nabokov—who did not compliment it, however."

Nabokov had his own second bite at the apple when he included his savaging of Arndt in his 1973 collection, *Strong Opinions*. Of Arndt's later editions, Nabokov sneered: "This 'revised' version still remains as abominable as before."[2]

WHEN EDMUND WILSON and Vladimir Nabokov met for the last time in January 1964 at Montreux, the weather was grim and there was too much drinking, Wilson lamented. Yet "it was all very merry and sparkling."

We don't know if the two men discussed Nabokov's *Onegin*, which would appear just six months later. Wilson was very much on the case. He had been sniffing around Bollingen since 1962, according to a letter from a staffer to the editor Anne Warren, preserved in the Nabokov archive:

For what it's worth, Edmund Wilson is dying to review Nabokov's *EO* and asked me when it was to be published. It seems
that he has already seen some of it in manuscript or something
(I didn't get whether he is a friend of Nabokov or not), and is
simply delighted with it. Seems he and N. have similar posi-
tions about the philosophy of translating.[3]

In May 1963, the Bollingen editor William McGuire informed
Nabokov that "we have had an inquiry from the new 'New York
Review of Books' asking about EO on behalf of Edmund Wilson.
It seems that he intends writing a long review for them, and he
would like to immerse himself in the matter over the summer."[4]

One can understand his excitement. Just as literature in New
York seemed to have ground to a standstill due to a printers' strike
at the *Times* and the other dailies, the *New York Review*, edited
by Robert Silvers and cofounded by Wilson's friends Jason and
Barbara Epstein, burst onto the scene with a welcome combination
of enthusiasm, erudition, and élan.* Buoyed by talented writers
sick of the hidebound *Times Book Review* and in some cases willing to write for free, the *Review* sold out the entire first print run
of what *The New Yorker* called "surely the best first issue of any
magazine ever."

Nabokov had scotched the idea of sending out prepublication
galleys, but McGuire wanted to make an exception for Wilson:

---

* Many felt that Elizabeth Hardwick's waspish 1959 *Harper's* essay, "The Decline
of Book Reviewing," set the table for *The New York Review*. Hardwick mercilessly
mocked the "unaccountable sluggishness" and "torpor" of the *Times's* book reviews.
To illustrate the prevailing cluelessness, she quoted the *Times* reviewer Orville
Prescott's offhand dismissal of Nabokov's runaway best seller: "*Lolita* is undeni-
ably news in the world of books. Unfortunately it is bad news." Hardwick went on
to write: "The condition of popular reviewing has become so listless, the effect of its
agreeable judgments so enervating to the general reading public that the sly publishers of *Lolita* have tried to stimulate sales by quoting *bad* reviews." (Hardwick and her
then-husband Robert Lowell also cofounded the *Review*.)

"We here feel strongly, however, that we should co-operate with Mr. Wilson. A review by him—in this new organ, which promises to be extremely influential—should have considerable impact. One of our advisers believes that it might increase sales by 500 or more."

Nabokov repeated his resolute *nyet* to sending out anything but completely finished *Onegin* copy: "I therefore suggest that we wait until we can supply Edmund Wilson with the final version of the complete text, and only in the case of an insuperable craving give him at least vol. 1 (complete and revised), vol. 2 (ditto) and the 1837 Russian text in page proof, *all in one batch.*"

As for reviews by distinguished commentators, Nabokov declared:

> I would like to add that I do not believe that a distinguished critic's review (or indeed any review) helps to sell a book. Readers are not sheep, and not every pen (pun) tempts them. Some of my best flops had been ushered in by extravagant (albeit well deserved) praise from eminent critics. The only thing that is of some help to the commercial success of a book (apart from topicality or sexuality) is a sustained advertising campaign, lots of ads everywhere.[5]

"I am not interested in the question of Edmund Wilson's writing or not writing about my EO," he concluded.

Shortly after the book was released in June, reviews started to appear. *The New York Times* loved it twice, in an appreciative squib by the legendary Moscow correspondent Harrison Salisbury ("He has given Pushkin's wondrous lines the glow and sparkle of their Russian original"), and in a lengthy Sunday excursus by Ernest Simmons, the Russian studies stalwart, ("Nabokov is

peculiarly attuned to the music and mystery of Pushkin's verse").
In a succinct but pointed *Los Angeles Times* review ("Nabokov
Fails as a Translator"), the scholar Stephen Nichols evinced little
use for this "voluminous compilation of fact and prejudice." The
unnamed, clearly fatigued *Boston Globe* reviewer praised the
work's "exhaustiveness": "If anything more remains to be uncov-
ered about Pushkin and *Onegin* it will be a surprise."

Nabokov cared little for the idle praise of nobodies. "Poor Simmons . . . is no scholar, and his knowledge of Russian has always
been very patchy," he wrote to Bollingen. Salisbury is "a well-
meaning journalist," but not someone to be taken very seriously,
and so on.

Nabokov's editors were hoping against hope that a prominent
Edmund Wilson review might move some product, but Nabokov
was chary, and suspicious. "The Foundation keeps looking forward to the Edmund Wilson article," he wrote in a 1964 letter,

> but as I have mentioned before his Russian is primitive, and his
> knowledge of Russian literature gappy and grotesque. (He is a
> very old friend of mine, and I do hope our quarter-of-a-century
> correspondence in the course of which I attempted not quite
> successfully to explain to him such matters as the mechanism
> of Russian—and English—verse will be published some day.)[6]

NOTA BENE: Edmund Wilson knew something about Alexander
Pushkin, and about his poetry. The world-famous, anathematiz-
ing Vladimir Nabokov would later make Wilson out to be the
dunce nonpareil of Russian letters, but that wasn't the case at all.
We saw Wilson trying to puzzle out some Pushkin in his Odessa
hospital bed in 1935, and two years later, on the hundredth anni-

versary of the poet's death, he published a lengthy tribute, "In Honor of Pushkin," in *The New Republic*. "I don't think you can give Pushkin too much space," Wilson wrote to the magazine's literary editor, Malcolm Cowley. "He was the greatest poet of the nineteenth century."[7]

Wilson's 1937 article is quite smart. It analyzes *Eugene Onegin* at some length, and places Pushkin right where he belongs, alongside Keats ("He can make us see and hear things as Keats can, but his range is very much greater") and Dante, and above many others ("much more vigorous than Jane Austen"). Wilson noted that Pushkin's work wasn't widely appreciated outside Russia because it was "particularly difficult to translate."

In the very thick of the two men's friendship, Wilson sent Nabokov the revised edition of his collection, *The Triple Thinkers*, which included the *New Republic* Pushkin essay. Nabokov pounced on what he called Wilson's "dreadful mistake" in retelling the crucial duel between Onegin and the feckless poet Vladimir Lensky. Wilson described the protagonists starting the encounter back-to-back, and walking away from each other, as "popularized by movies and cartoons," according to Nabokov. "This variant did not exist in Pushkin's Russia," Nabokov scolded. The actual format was the French "duel à volonté" with the combatants facing each other from about thirty paces apart. Wilson corrected his account in later editions of the book.[8]

In his early forties, with the memory of Russia and the timbre of the language still fresh in his ear, Wilson was besotted by Pushkin. He loved Babette Deutsch's and Avrahm Yarmolinsky's 1937 *Onegin* translation, telling them, "It was a heroic feat to have carried it through in the original meter and rhyme scheme!"[9] Wilson even dreamed of Pushkin. In a 1937 letter to his longtime friend, the poet Louise Bogan, he wrote: "I had a dream the other night in which I thought I was reading a poem by Pushkin about a trout: he addressed the trout as 'little fox,' which seemed to me very apt."[10]

A few years later Wilson wrote a second essay on Pushkin, for *The Atlantic Monthly,* praising "the texture of Pushkin's language and its marvelous adaptation to whatever it describes. . . . The timing in Pushkin is perfect. He never for a moment bores you," Wilson wrote, "yet he covers an immense amount of ground."[11] This appeared in 1943, after he and Nabokov had known each other for three years. Was Wilson cribbing from his Russian friend? One critic thought so. Stanley Edgar Hyman accused Wilson of using "many of the specific insights of Vladimir Nabokov, whose translations he has been working with for several years." In a 1948 book Hyman added that "Wilson is quite possibly indebted to Nabokov for the remarkable and quite uncharacteristic, detailed analysis of musicality in a poem by Pushkin he printed in his Pushkin article in the *Atlantic Monthly,* an analysis that seems to represent a remarkable acquaintance with the Russian language on Wilson's part and seems at the same time very characteristic of Nabokov."[12]

All this to say that Wilson must have been genuinely interested in what Nabokov proposed to do with, or to, *Onegin.* He finally got his hands on the book after its publication in June 1964. Writing from Wellfleet in June, he told the *New York Review* editor Barbara Epstein that he planned to spend the summer with the book in Talcottville, "go through it very carefully," and have his review ready in a few months. "Just looking through it," he wrote, "I can see that Volodya's translation is almost as much open to objection as Arndt's. It is full of flat writing, outlandish words, and awkward phrases. And some of the things he says about the Russian language are inaccurate."[13]

Wilson's long-awaited, 6,600-word review, "The Strange Case of Pushkin and Nabokov," finally appeared in July 1965, more than a year after *Onegin*'s publication. It remains a classic of its genre, the genre being an overlong, spiteful, stochastically accurate, generally useless but unfailingly amusing hatchet job, the yawning, massive load of boiling pitch that inevitably ends up scalding the grinning fiend pouring the hot oil over the battlement as much as it harms the intended victim.

Setting the tone for the ensuing seven-plus years of malicious rhetoric, Wilson reminded *New York Review* readers that he and Nabokov were "personal friends" and that he remained "an admirer of much of his work." Recalling that Nabokov had tap-danced over Arndt in those very pages, Wilson wrote that Nabokov's own *Onegin* ventures "have been more disastrous than those of Arndt's heroic effort."

How so? Let us count the ways.

• *Recondite vocabulary:* "The only characteristic Nabokov trait that one recognizes in this uneven and sometimes banal translation is the addiction to rare and unfamiliar words." Examples, please? Wilson is glad you asked: "rememorating, producement, curvate, habitude, rummers, familistic, gloam, dit, shippon and scrab," to name just a few. (Did he miss "catopromantic"?) Wilson inquired, reasonably, why Nabokov had translated "monkeys" as "sapajous," "langour" as "mollitude," and what in heaven's name is "stuss"? "Nabokov's aberrations in this line are a good deal more objectionable than anything I have found in Arndt," Wilson concluded.

• *Broken English:* "I have never seen the word *loadened* before, and I had found, on looking it up . . . that it is not a past participle, as Nabokov makes it." "The past of *dwell* is *dwelt* not *dwelled*"; " 'Remind one about me' is hardly English."

And what, Wilson asked, is Tatiana supposed to be saying here, as she bids farewell to her country home (7.32)?: "Farewell pacific sites/Farewell secluded refuge!/Shall I see you?" "Such passages sound like the products of those computers which are supposed to translate Russian into English," according to Wilson.

· *I know Russian, too:* Wilson launched what would become a multi-year debate about the gerund *pochuya,* which means "sniffing" or "smelling," if you are a horse. Wilson rolled out seven different dictionaries* to buttress his insistence on "smelling." (Nabokov had sniffed at Wilson's horse "sniffing" in the footnote where he derided his former friend's 1936 translation effort.) Nabokov translated the line as the "naggy having sensed the snow," "an egregious example of his style at its most perversepedantic impossible," according to Wilson. One's heart goes out to the tired spines of the reference works in the two men's respective homes, clearly in need of bibliorthopedic intervention.

· *I know Russian, too, II:* Several of Wilson's friends, most notably his Wellfleet neighbor Nina Chavchavadze, warned him not to engage Nabokov on his home turf. Wilson's Russian was fine, for an outlander, and yes, he doggedly burrowed into the appropriate reference works, but still. Nabokov doesn't know the meaning of *nyetu* ("no," or "none"), Wilson insisted. Nabokov errs when he writes that *zloi* (evil) is the only one-syllable adjective in Russian. What about—and Wilson named several others in current use. He accused Nabokov of muffing his explanation of the Russian *e* topped with a diaeresis, which is pronounced "yo." (The classic example being the name Khrushchev, which Russians

---

* "... the small Müller-Boyanus dictionary and two others ... Segal's larger dictionary ... Daum and Schenk's Die Russischen Verben ... The great Russian dictionary of V. I. Dahl ... The Soviet Pushkin Dictionary."

properly pronounce "Khroosh-CHYOFF," or Potemkin, actually "Pot-YOM-kin.")

Wilson is overextending himself here, to put it gently. But, in · the manner of Napoleon's favorite generals, he presses forward, nothing loath. *Toujours l'audace!*

"In a tedious and interminable appendix"—we are about 3,200 words into the critique by now—"Nabokov expounds a system of prosody, also invented by himself." For a quarter century, each man had proclaimed himself to be an expert on the intricacies of scansion, pronunciation, and phonometrics, to borrow Arndt's term, of Russian and English verse. "Edmund Wilson never did learn how the Russian stress system, metrics or prosody work," Simon Karlinsky wrote long after both men were dead.[14]

Yet another theme: *Nabokov longa, Pushkin brevis.* Addressing Nabokov's crazy tutorial on "racemosa," Wilson wrote: "This is the Nabokov we know. The Nabokov who bores and fatigues by overaccumulation." By contrast, "no poet surpasses Pushkin—not even Dante—for the speed, point and neatness of his narrative."

"And now for the positive side," Wilson wrote, with the end in sight. But the positive would have to wait. Instead Wilson chose to pull yet another bone out of the muck, a long-running dispute about Pushkin's knowledge, or ignorance, of English. It's an interesting question, because Pushkin was nothing if not Byronesque, and he once called *Onegin* "a novel in verse in the manner of Byron's *Don Juan*,"[15] which shares a discursive narrative style with its Russian counterpart. Nabokov dogmatically insisted that Pushkin didn't know much English and had read Byron only in French, evidence to the contrary notwithstanding. Wilson noted that Pushkin's notebooks quoted passages from, and whole English poems by, Wordsworth, Coleridge, and Byron, among others.

"Nabokov himself notes that Pushkin had English books in his library, but asserts that he could not read them," Wilson wrote. Another sticking point.*

What about the positive side? "There is a good deal of excellent literary criticism" buried in Nabokov's nineteen hundred pages, Wilson allowed. "When Nabokov is not being merely snide and silly but taking his subject seriously, he gives us excellent little essays." Furthermore, Nabokov abhors talk of literary "schools," Wilson wrote, and so do I.

It seemed inevitable that Wilson's symphony of bile and sly diggery would build to a climactic crescendo, and it does. "There is a drama in [Nabokov's] *Eugene Onegin* which is not Onegin's drama," Wilson concluded. "It is the drama of Nabokov himself attempting to correlate his English and his Russian sides." "Not quite at home with Russia," Nabokov, per Wilson, shows with his stilted literal translation of *Onegin* that "what he writes is not always really English."

Poor Vladimir. An exile. An orphan. A stranger to two worlds, and in two languages. A Conrad manqué. Wilson was trafficking in precisely the kind of "human interest" twaddle that Nabokov reviled.

After reading Wilson's piece at home in Montreux, Nabokov cabled Barbara Epstein in New York: "Please reserve space in next issue for my thunder."

---

* Two recent Pushkin biographers agree with Wilson. David Bethea writes that "by approximately 1828 . . . Pushkin's English was sufficient to read both Byron and Shakespeare in the original." T. J. Binyon concurs, noting that Pushkin had extensive contacts with English writers and translated English poetry for his magazine *The Contemporary*.

8

We Are All Pushkinists Now

And so it began. The exchanges, which endured after both men's deaths, were achingly serious and gloriously silly, catnip for editors who liked sprightly "knocking copy," as the British call disputatious texts. There was plenty of it, free for the asking. The rival campaigns evoke Marshal Kutuzov reeling his forces backward in defense of Moscow, only to rally them forward again, staggering, against Murat's serried and exhausted Frenchmen.

When Nabokov wearied of exchanging blows in *The New York Review*, he staged a massive attack in Stephen Spender's *Encounter* magazine, shortly to be exposed as a CIA front. (Which doubtless concerned Nabokov not one whit.) Arcane, brief-lived skirmishes erupted in the *New Statesman*, avidly read by both Nabokov and Wilson, and finally in *The New York Times Book Review*. Sooner or later a motley crew of 1960s eminentos—Anthony Burgess, Robert Lowell, V. S. Pritchett, Robert Graves, and Paul Fussell, among many others—dipped their oars in the roiled Sargasso of Pushkin criticism. A subject, it's fair to say, about which most of them knew absolutely nothing.

Jeffrey Meyers aptly compares the Wilson-Nabokov hostilities to a carefully choreographed nineteenth-century duel, with its balletic rules. Wilson had fired his LePage pistol, stuffed full of raking shot, in July 1965. Now Nabokov, like the prostrate Pushkin wounded by his enemy D'Anthès's opening salvo, was entitled to return fire.

So in August the *Review* printed Nabokov's suspiciously short reply, with a brief rejoinder from Wilson, along with six letters from readers, known and unknown. Professor Ernest Simmons popped up again, to point out that Nabokov had succeeded in translating a few of Pushkin's verses into rhyming stanzas, and "might have succeeded brilliantly" had he honored the *Onegin* stanza form throughout. Writing from London, the renowned translator David Magarshack "warmly agreed . . . with Edmund Wilson's views of Nabokov's incompetence as a translator. In fact, his 'translation' of Eugene Onegin is a grotesque travesty of that great poem." Magarshack was precisely the kind of mainstream translator Nabokov disdained. Suffice it to say that Magarshack did not title his classic 1968 translation of Dostoyevsky's *Notes from the Underground* "Memoirs from a Mousehole," which Nabokov regarded as a more accurate translation.

Comes now the thunder. Nabokov acceded to Wilson's observation that the two men "are indeed old friends. . . . In the 1940s, during my first decade in America, he was most kind to me in various matters." A kindness that Nabokov felt had long since been repaid, partly in the form of free Russian lessons from the master:

A patient confidant of his long and hopeless infatuation with the Russian language, I have always done my best to explain to him his mistakes of pronunciation, grammar, and interpretation. As late as 1957, at one of our last meetings, we both realized with amused dismay that despite my frequent comments on Russian prosody, he still could not scan Russian verse.

That's no crime. But this is:

Upon being challenged to read *Eugene Onegin* aloud, he started to do this with great gusto, garbling every second word and turning Pushkin's iambic line into a kind of spastic anapest with a lot of jaw-twisting haws and rather endearing little barks that utterly jumbled the rhythm and soon had us both in stitches.

After promising to publish "a complete account of the bizarre views on the art of translation" shared among his critics, Nabokov said that Wilson's critique "will then receive all the friendly attention it deserves." Nabokov proceeded to unpack about a dozen of Wilson's Russian-language errors, sarcastic commentary very much included. "I do not think Mr. Wilson should try to teach me how to pronounce this or any other Russian vowel. . . . This is Mr. Wilson showing me how to translate properly," and so on. Several of these points of contention will be revisited for the next several years: Is *netu* archaic? (Yes and no.) Is the card game "stuss" in the English dictionary? (Yes, in the *OED*.) Should Wilson have dialed back his gassy lecture on the gerund *pochuya*, that cursed "naggy" sniffing again? (Yes, he should have.)*

Wilson sneaked two separate, thousand-word missives into the

* In one of the few letters *not* printed by the *Review* (but filed in Wilson's papers) a Russian instructor from Reed College challenged Wilson's analysis of *pochuya*: "This class of perfective adverbial participles ending in –a (-ja) is discussed in [sections] 820–822 of the first volume of *Grammatika russkogo jazyka* published in 1960 by the Soviet Academy of Sciences."

Review before the end of the year, adding little if anything to the discussion. He had, alas, been proved wrong on several points, which prompted a modest climbdown: "It is just as well that Mr. Nabokov should be able to tax me with these mistakes, for, in rereading my article, I felt that it sounded more damaging than I had meant it to be, and this has given him a chance to score." Nonetheless, Wilson continued to argue fine points of prosody and pronunciation with his unseen adversary. He tried to hide behind distinctions between "U" and "non-U" Russian, which feels like reaching. Then he revisited Gerundistan, trying to dig himself out of his mistranslation of the sniffing "naggy": "For the benefit of other strugglers with this expressive but preposterous language, it should be said that since *pochuyat'* is a perfective verb . . . [it] can have only a past meaning."

Nabokov was silent. Had he left the battlefield? No, the wily chess master had opened a second front.* And here it is: the nuclear option, a 4,500-word-long "Reply to My Critics," published in London's *Encounter* magazine.[1] *Encounter* might be deemed home ground. Editor Spender was friendly with both Vladimir and his cousin Nicolas Nabokov—he was also quite friendly with Wilson—and the magazine had printed Anthony Burgess's long, serious, and elegiac review of Nabokov's *Onegin* a few months earlier. Burgess was no stranger to Russian wordplay and the trickeries of translation, having invented the proto-Russian language "nadsat' " for the violent marauders of his 1962 novel, *A Clockwork Orange*. He coined "Droog" for the Russian *droug*, or "friend"; the Korova ("Cow") Milk Bar; and the like.

In his review Burgess tried his own hand at translating *Onegin*

* Actually Nabokov was hoping to wage war on two fronts simultaneously; he offered the *Encounter* rant to Barbara Epstein at *The New York Review*, but she declined to publish it.

and decided that it was difficult indeed. "These four volumes . . . represent the very perfection of scholarship," he concluded. Nabokov's *Onegin*, he wrote, "itself approaches great art."

Now, a few months later, in his "Reply to My Critics," Nabokov quickly cleared out some underbrush. Professor Guy Daniels's bitchy *New Republic* review was "prompted by a sordid little grudge," he insisted.* A *Noviy Zhurnal* critic was an idiot who can't speak Russian, and didn't read my book anyway. The *Los Angeles Times* reviewer fails utterly, etc. But "the longest, most ambitious, most captious, and, alas, most reckless article is Mr. Edmund Wilson's in *The New York Review of Books* and this I now select for a special examination."

So this is the comprehensive, "friendly attention" that Nabokov had previously promised. Nabokov recycled some earlier insults, for example, Wilson's "turning Pushkin's iambic line into a kind of spastic anapest" into this latest article. He again derided Wilson's knowledge of Russian, revisiting the pronunciation of the vowel *yo*, looking in on the gerund *pochuya* for now the fourth time, and cruelly mocked Wilson's assertion that Nabokov had said that there is only one one-syllable adjective in Russian: "Every time Mr. Wilson starts examining a Russian phrase he makes some ludicrous slip."

It is an inconvenient truth that there are several one-syllable adjectives in Russian, but we move on.

---

* In a letter to his Bollingen editor William McGuire, Nabokov elaborated on the "private grudge": "In 1962 Daniels coolly named me as a sponsor when applying for a Guggenheim fellowship. The Foundation asked me for details and I wrote back saying I had never given G.D. the permission to use my name, and that anyway I disapproved of his translation (wretched rhymed paraphrases.)" Whatever his motives, Daniels ridiculed Nabokov's *Onegin*, calling out "monstrosities of 'non-English' verging on gibberish, outright mistranslations and total lapses of sensitivity." He mocked Nabokov's "Man-Dog-Bite Word Order," for example, "But portends bereavements/the pitiful tune of this dit [*sic*]," and caught the master in a couple of infelicities that prompted minor changes in the second edition.

There follow about a thousand words of (one-sided) debate over the accusation that Nabokov is "[addicted] to rare and unfamiliar words." What this boils down to is Nabokov's championing of *Webster's Third International Dictionary, Unabridged*, "which I really must urge Mr. Wilson to acquire," and Wilson's reliance on the *Oxford English Dictionary*. Words like "curvate," "habitude," "rememorate," "familistic," "scrab," "loaden," and yes, "mollitude," are in my dictionary, so bugger off, Nabokov wrote.* Then he twice revisited the issue of Pushkin's knowledge of English, insisting that "my demonstration remains unassailable" and that "Mr. Wilson knows nothing about the question."

Then there is the charge of infelicity. Wilson had accused Nabokov of mimicking computer translations with phrases like "Very nicely did our pal act" (4.18). The English seems indefensible, but Nabokov insisted that "the corresponding Russian was also trite and trivial." As for "Farewell, pacific sites!/Farewell, secluded refuge!/Shall I see you?" Nabokov insisted that Tatiana is speaking "in a stilted and old-fashioned idiom" and he was merely following her lead.

In the end it was more—and yet more—of the same. Nabokov summarized Wilson's article as "entirely consisting, as I have shown, of quibbles and blunders, can be damaging only to his own reputation—and that is the last look I shall ever take at the dismal scene."

Even Wilson sounded fatigued in an uncharacteristically brief rejoinder: "Mr. Nabokov is hissing and shrieking again . . ." Wilson didn't quite understand Nabokov's brusque venue shifting; I answered these questions in *The New York Review*, he wrote,

---

* When he republished the "Reply" in a 1973 collection, Nabokov noted that "rememorated" had disappeared from the revised edition of *Onegin*, "for reasons having nothing to do with the subject of this essay."

and "I don't propose to recapitulate here. . . . There is no need to discuss the absurd justifications for the absurdities of the Nabokov translation." Schoolboy Wilson cannot resist a final dig. "The word 'byre,' by the way, is not American, but British," he writes. "This error has not only doubled me up with mirth, it has caused me to roll on the floor exsufficate with cachinnation."

At an academic conference I learned the old adage that everything has been said, but not everyone has said it. And so it was here. A raft of opinionated if not well-informed literary types crawled forth from the woodwork to support either Wilson or Nabokov. Robert Lowell, who would have been America's poet laureate, if America had had such a thing in 1966, decided to dip his patrician paw in the barrel. Although self-avowedly "a reader with no Russian," Lowell was not a reader with no point of view, and his was decidedly anti-Nabokov. Calling him a "zany genius," Lowell said that what he "has written is a weirdly eccentric minor English poem, one that suggests that Pushkin's *Onegin* is not, as everyone claims, a national classic, but some wildly queer miscarriage. . . . Both commonsense and intuition tell us that Edmund Wilson must be nine-tenths unanswerable and right in his criticism of Nabokov," Lowell wrote. "The long arguments about Russian gerunds, the devious dictionary meanings of Russian and English words, etc., cannot conceal what is obvious, that Nabokov's *Onegin* is really, and perhaps only half intentionally, a spoof at its readers, rival translators, Pushkin, and Nabokov himself."

Eight years' worth of work and five thousand index cards . . . a spoof?! Hold that thought.

Spender gave Nabokov some space to kiss off Lowell: "He does not know Pushkin's language and is not equipped to tackle the special problems of translation discussed." Nabokov voiced his wish that Lowell "would stop mutilating defenceless dead poets—

Mandelshtam, Rimbaud and others." This referred to Lowell's celebrated "imitations," in which he recast a famous poem based on a literal translation by a native language speaker. Lowell's collection *Imitations* won, yes, the Bollingen Poetry Translation Prize in 1962.*

The eminent novelist, poet, and translator Robert Graves found his way into *Encounter*'s pages, expressing his admiration for Nabokov, "a precisian in the rich Russian language and . . . a precisian in the equally rich and even more widely dispersed English language." Graves voiced "regret to see him quarreling with Mr. Edmund Wilson, one of the ablest prose writers in the United States, however gross the provocation."

In a nutshell Graves agreed with Wilson that Nabokov was guilty of using crackpot vocabulary, for example, "dit" for "ditty" or "song"; "loaden" for "laden"; and "curvate," which Graves huffed "is not in the *O.E.D.*, and we do not know Noah Webster's source for its use." It's far from clear which end of the proverbial stick Graves is brandishing, however, because he misunderstood Wilson's (and Nabokov's editors') objection to the use of "pal." Graves thought the pal was a woman: "Maybe 'miss' is the right word for the *Eugene Onegin* context." Not exactly.

To Nabokov's great delight—and to Wilson's apparent chagrin— *Onegin*-related brushfires kept flaring up in unexpected places. The thirty-one-year-old Christopher Ricks, Oxford's future Pro-

---

* Nabokov treated Lowell to the Full Vladimir in a memorable *New York Review* dressing-down in 1969. Olga Carlisle ("Miss Carlisle" to Nabokov, ignoring her marital status), the granddaughter of the Russian writer Leonid Andreyev, had commissioned Lowell to translate Soviet-era poets, reworking her own, literal—that is, *Onegin*-like—translations. "If this kind of thing becomes an international fashion," Nabokov fumed, "I can easily imagine Robert Lowell himself finding one of his best poems . . . adapted in some other country by some eminent, blissfully monolingual foreign poet, assisted by some American expatriate with a not too extensive vocabulary in any language."

fessor of Poetry, praised the new *Onegin* in the *New Statesman*. Ricks clearly warmed to Nabokov's "crotchety, superbly opinionated, humiliatingly erudite" translation, which he compared favorably to that of Babette Deutsch. Ms. Deutsch was a favorite Nabokov punching bag, whose translations Wilson had praised.

A seemingly innocent reader wrote a letter to the *Statesman*, questioning Ricks's preference. That did not go unnoticed on the sixth floor of the Montreux Palace Hotel. Nabokov made short shrift of Deutsch's hapless "paraphrase" of Pushkin, which in turn prompted a response to the *New Statesman* from Deutsch herself. In a brief note Deutsch demurely suggested that the reader compare her mellifluous lines about the peasant's horse sniffing the new snow with Nabokov's ham-handed account of the shambling "naggy." That odd word, she explained, did indeed appear in *The Shorter OED*, and it means "given to nagging."

What could have delighted Nabokov more? Not only had Deutsch not sued him for libel, as the skittish Bollingen editors had fretted she might, but she had emerged onto open ground to do battle.

Yet again Nabokov defended his naggy, not bothering to plump the obvious superiority of his elephantine Webster's dictionary over the puny *OED*. He derided her pleasant, lilting line (Deutsch was a poet of some renown) "His mare scents snow upon the pleasant/Keen air." There is no pleasant keen air in the original, Nabokov wrote; it has been piped in by Ms. Deutsch. And there's no mare there, he pointed out. In Russian the horse's gender was undetermined. There was a pun to be had, though: "Miss Deutsch's version is little more than a nightmare."

For whatever reason the novelist and critic V. S. Pritchett decided he wanted a piece of this action. At the end of a review of David Magarshack's biography *Pushkin*, Pritchett alluded to the "diverting dispute between Nabokov and Edmund Wilson," and wondered out loud why Magarshack didn't address the burning question of Pushkin's knowledge of English: "Is it true that he could have read Byron only in French?"

More raw meat for Nabokov, who believed he had resolved this question once and for all in his *Onegin* "Commentary": "I suggest [Pritchett] consult the pages . . . wherein I explain, quite clearly, that most Russians of Pushkin's time, including Pushkin himself, read English authors in French versions."

But Wilson hadn't let his *Statesman* subscription lapse. "Mr. Nabokov's insolently imperious tone seems sometimes to impress readers who know nothing of the subject in dispute," he wrote in a letter to the magazine, and then trotted out, again, the considerable evidence that Pushkin had a working knowledge of Byron's English. "Mr. Nabokov, as I have often noticed, seems to be determined to 'demonstrate' . . . that he is the only Russian writer who has ever mastered English."

Wilson repeated Nabokov's statement that Pushkin, "like most Russians . . . was poor at languages," and mocked it. How, he asked, would Nabokov know? He hadn't been to Russia in decades, and was apparently unaware that "since the Revolution there have been a good many young Russians who, without ever having left their country, have learned to speak English or French almost as fluently . . . as Mr. Nabokov himself."[2]

Magarshack was living in London, so his magazine arrived promptly. "Reluctant as I am to intervene in the dispute between two such redoubtable opponents as Mr. Vladimir Nabokov and Mr. Edmund Wilson . . ." Then intervene he did. Citing "my recently published biography of Pushkin," Magarshack dredged up a Russian army officer "said to have perfect knowledge of English," who heard Pushkin read and translate Shakespeare. The poet's pronunciation "was somewhat eccentric, and when challenged on that point he laughed and said he read English as if it were Latin."

Pushkin's translation, the officer reported, was "absolutely correct and his understanding of the language irreproachable."

Nabokov, who was losing ground on this point, wrote in that he wasn't so interested in fighting after all: "Sir: I do not intend to continue my chats with Mr. Edmund Wilson, in private or in print, but let me humbly concede before ending them, that Pushkin had almost as much English in the 1830s as Mr. Edmund Wilson has Russian today. That should satisfy everybody."[3]

Are we done? Not quite. An interesting character shambles into our drama, a personage of almost Gogolian gravamen: the Harvard professor Alexander Gerschenkron, like Nabokov an émigré intellectual from the upper stratum of pre-Revolutionary Russia. Gerschenkron's nominal field was economic history, but he was an omnididact of gargantuan reach, known around Harvard as "the Great Gerschenkron." At a university where self-regard flows like mother's milk through the hallways, Gerschenkron was a mythic figure. He purported to have wooed Marlene Dietrich (quite possibly), to have played chess with Marcel Duchamp (true—he lost), and boasted of an apparently fictional friendship with the Boston Red Sox left fielder Ted Williams—who, we can safely assume, was unaware of his existence. Gerschenkron famously feared no one. Not the Bolsheviks, not the Nazis, not his liberal sparring partner John Kenneth Galbraith, and certainly not Vladimir Nabokov.

An intellectual of the old school, Gerschenkron knew Pushkin inside and out. Like many Russians, he could recite massive swatches of *Onegin* by heart. Nabokov was a known quantity at Harvard. He had worked as a research fellow at the Museum of Comparative Zoology from 1942 to 1948, helping to catalog the university's considerable collections of rare butterflies. Visiting from Cornell, Nabokov haunted Harvard's superb libraries, researching the *Onegin* "Commentary," and he guest-taught several times, sitting in for his friends, the Slavic scholar Mikhail Karpovich and Harry Levin. Gerschenkron didn't much like Nabokov, and he especially disliked what Nabokov had done to *Onegin*. And, unlike Wilson, this was not an away game for Gerschenkron. The gallicisms, the prosody, the archaic Slavic roots of Pushkin's vocabulary were as familiar to him as they were to Nabokov.

Gerschenkron's ten-thousand-word critique in *Modern Philology* began at a deceptively slow pace:

> Vladimir Nabokov's monumental edition of *Eugene Onegin* is the strangest blend, fascinating and exasperating. It has everything: artistic intuition and dogmatic stubbornness; great ingenuity and amazing folly; acute observations and sterile pedantry; unnecessary modesty and inexcusable arrogance. It is a labor of love and a work of hate.

Clearing his throat, Gerschenkron attacked several of Nabokov's by-now-better-known solecisms: translating "monkey" as "sapajou"; *tsvetky*, or "little flowers," as "flowerets"; rosy lips became "vermeil lips"; and so on. Because Nabokov was seeking approximations for Pushkin's rolling iambs, Gerschenkron wrote, "Russian fur coats become 'pelisses,' 'curses' become imprecations and old peasant women have acquired the vocabulary of college students."

Gerschenkron admired a few of Nabokov's lines, but warned that "such lovely flowers are surrounded, if not smothered, by much less fragrant weeds." There was a malodorous infestation of malapropisms in this *Onegin*. Gerschenkron cited this one (6.3), among others:

With his un-looked-for apparition,
the momentary softness of his eyes
and odd conduct with Olga,
to the depth of her soul
she's penetrated.

Gerschenkron's preliminary conclusion: "Nabokov's translation can and should be studied, but . . . it cannot be read."

Finding his stride, Gerschenkron offered examples of "the author's uncontrolled anger, his lack of generosity, his narrow prejudices, eccentricities, inconsistencies and irrelevancies." To wit: "Insipid Vergil and his pale pederasts"; "Voltaire's abominably pedestrian verses"; "the well-meaning but *talentlos* August Wilhelm Schlegel"—and fourteen more such examples. "This, no doubt, was great stuff *pour épater la coed* at Cornell," Gerschenkron noted, adding that "it has no bearing at all on *Eugene Onegin* or Pushkin in general. . . . Nabokov is out to cut throats."

Gerschenkron praised the "probable" accuracy of the "Commentary," then let slip that he had bothered to check only one of Nabokov's references. It proved to be a mis-citation of Juvenal, which Nabokov was forced to correct in the 1975 edition. That the one footnote he checked proved to be wrong, Gerschenkron ascribed to "just my own bad luck." He also cited many other errors, for example, a wrong date; German grammar contorted; a city was east, not west, of Odessa. Trivial slips to be sure, the professor noted, yet these are precisely the motes that Nabokov so gleefully exposed in the eyes of his rivals.

There were other gems along the way. When Gerschenkron

wanted to cite a more euphonic translation, he turned to Walter
Arndt. Hacking through the underbrush of the "Pedal Digression," he drolly noted that "it is, incidentally, odd that Lolita's
bard, a nymphet's singer," should rule out the possibility of an
affair between Pushkin and the thirteen-and-a-half-year-old
Maria Rayevskaya, "since Pushkin had some proclivities in that
direction." He then cited and footnoted two instances of Pushkin
dallying with twelve- and thirteen-year-old girls.

Most convincingly, Gerschenkron indicted Nabokov for mean-
ness of spirit, for failing to celebrate the reflected beauty of Pushkin's glorious poem in the work of the many scholars who had
enriched the collective understanding of Onegin. We know, for
instance, that Pushkin enciphered fragments of the unpublished
chapter 10. Nabokov had written that "[Pyotr] Morozov easily
broke the clumsy code" in question. "This patronizing tone about
the major achievement of a scholar," Gerschenkron wrote, "comes
with exceedingly poor grace from a writer who is ever ready to
exult over his own little discoveries."

This was the critique that Wilson should have written, but
could not. Gerschenkron had the Russian, the French, the German, and a Nabokovian self-confidence in his grasp of Onegin.
Wilson, who had a nodding, sidewalks-of-Cambridge acquaintance with Gerschenkron, realized this at once. He quickly dashed
off a note to the academic:

[Your article] is the best thing, the only really thoroughgoing
study. I tried to do something about it, but, on the Russian end,
was not so well equipped as you. I wonder whether Nabokov
has seen it. He was furious about my piece. Like all people who
play practical jokes and like to make other people ridiculous,

he's always either aggrieved or indignant when anybody tries anything of the kind on him.[4]

Nicholas Dawidoff, Gershenkron's grandson, wrote a brisk and admiring biography of his ancestor, *The Fly Swatter: How My Grandfather Made His Way in the World*. Describing this incident, Dawidoff pointed out that "Nabokov had made a point of answering and rebutting every last critic of the translation that had taken so many years of his life, but in [Gerschenkron]'s case he did not reply." Dawidoff quotes the Slavicist and Nabokov specialist Alexander Dolinin saying that "I noticed that all the objections and notions of Gerschenkron were so correct that Nabokov quietly made all of Gerschenkron's corrections when he put out his second edition of *Eugene Onegin*."[5]

Nabokov thought that the merciless Gerschenkron takedown might have been a Harvard hit—and that Wilson had his finger near the trigger. Nabokov learned that Wilson had passed the article on to their mutual friend Roman Grynberg for publication in a Russian journal that Grynberg edited. Nabokov to Grynberg, February 1976: "About Gerschenkron: His article is far from innocent (it was written, with the most vulgar grimaces, in defense of Harvard's [Dmitri] Chizhevsky, whom I ruffled with good reason), and you can tell Wilson from me, that in passing it on he's a scoundrel."

It is probably no coincidence, as the Marxists like to say, that Chizhevsky was a member of the Prague Linguistic Circle, alongside Roman Jakobson, who became a Harvard celebrity. Jakobson, like Nabokov a finely honed talent who sprang from an affluent, pre-Revolutionary background, was one of Nabokov's bêtes noires. At a famous Cambridge dinner party hosted by Harry

Levin in 1952, Nabokov forgot, or pretended to forget, Jakobson's patronymic, a cheap insult in Russian etiquette. That same evening Levin's young daughter tape-recorded both men reading Pushkin. When Jakobson inflicted his Moscow accent on the Petersburg poet, Nabokov audibly commented, *"Eto uzhasno"* ["That's awful"].[6]

A few years later Nabokov formally broke with Jakobson while the two men were collaborating on a translation of the folk poem *The Song of Igor's Campaign.* Jakobson traveled to the USSR and maintained ties with Soviet academicians, a line that Nabokov refused to cross. "Frankly, I am unable to stomach your little trips to totalitarian countries," Nabokov wrote in 1957, "even if these trips are prompted by scientific considerations." "Nabokov was in fact convinced that Jakobson was a communist agent," according to the biographer Brian Boyd.

In 1957 Jakobson scotched Nabokov's chance to become a Harvard professor. When a small groundswell, nurtured in part by Harry Levin, emerged to offer Nabokov tenure in the Slavic Languages and Literature Department, Jakobson, the chairman, uttered the quote heard 'round the Yard: "Gentlemen, even if one allows that he is an important writer, are we next to invite an elephant to be Professor of Zoology?" Soon afterward Hurricane Lolita blew Nabokov to the Alps, where he became more famous, and richer, than an entire Fellows Table of Harvard professors.

Nabokov had a vengeful nature, and avenge himself he did. In his 1969 novel, *Ada,* there appears a hapless academic, "Dr Gerschizhevsky." "Vivian Darkbloom"'s footnote explains that "a Slavist's name gets mixed here with that of Chizhevski, another Slavist." (Vivian Darkbloom, a famous anagram of Vladimir Nabokov, is also a character in *Lolita*.) Nabokov had borrowed the names of two of his least favorite scholars—Gerschenkron and

Chizhevsky—both of Harvard, and lampooned them in his best-selling book. Chizhevsky, himself the author of an *Onegin* commentary, had already taken quite a buffeting from Nabokov, who at different moments in his "Commentary" derided Chizhevsky's work as "careless," "stumbling," and "worthless."

When *The New York Times* asked Gerschenkron about his unwilling cameo in *Ada*, he called it "a small man's revenge."

This is not, to steal Nabokov's line, the last look we shall take at this dismal scene.

9

Until Death Do Us Part

The epistolary clashes over *Onegin* had wound down by the end of 1967. Wilson and Nabokov had suspended their correspondence. However, Nabokov did like to scratch the itch. In October 1966, he wrote to Page Stegner, an English professor at Ohio State who was compiling *The Portable Nabokov:* "You have a perfect right to quote Edmund Wilson on my contempt for ignoramuses but your readers might have liked to be told that . . . I *proved* him one."[1] A few months later, Vera asked Stegner to include Vladimir's *Encounter* broadside, "Reply to My Critics" in the compendium: "The inclusion of this piece V.N. considers very important because Mr. Wilson furtively continues his personal attacks."

Nabokov continued to play his little tricks. In the thick of the *Onegin* war he was reediting and embellishing his 1951 memoir, *Speak, Memory*, which could be counted on to sell thousands more copies now that its author was world famous. In the revision Nabokov compared his childhood inability to capture a rare butterfly to the "absurd oversight" in chess made by the "world-famous grandmaster Wilhelm Edmundson" during a match with the "local amateur and pediatrician, Dr. Schach, who eventually won." Professor Elizabeth Sweeney deserves credit for solving this intricate puzzle. Schach is a dig at the popular pediatrician, Dr. Benjamin Spock, and also the German word for "chess" (and the Russian word for "check," in chess). Noticing that Nabokov's butterfly has "a white W on its . . . underside," Sweeney writes, "invites the careful reader to transpose the syllables of the name 'Wilhelm Edmundson.' "[2]

More prosaically, there was no world-famous grandmaster of that name.

In the Wilson household, Nabokov remained very much on the radar. The two men often laundered their opinions and accusations through their common friend Roman Grynberg, a businessman and publisher who had known and liked both writers since the 1930s. In prebreakup 1962, Wilson shared his opinion of Nabokov's novel *Pale Fire* with Grynberg, but not with the author. "Have you seen Volodya's new book?" Wilson inquired. "I read it with amusement, but it seems to me rather silly. Do let me know what you think of it. I expected that the professor would turn out to be the real King and that the commentator would be the assassin; but he doesn't seem to have had this idea. . . . The book must have been inspired by his own commentary in *Onegin*."*

Nabokov's next new novel was *Ada*, and Wilson again shared his opinion with the Grynbergs. "Have you people read Volodya's new novel? I am just about to do so. I understand that he takes a nasty crack at me in it." Indeed he did. Sweeney decoded yet another anti-Wilson dig, this time buried in "Vivian Darkbloom" 's notes at the end of *Ada*. Darkbloom explains that the

---

* The mad, erudite Frederick Exley devoted the better part of his second book, *Pages From a Cold Island*, to Wilson. Exley indulged the surprising opinion—unique to him—that John Shade, the nominal poet-creator of *Pale Fire*, was closely modeled on Nabokov's then-friend Wilson.

chess player identified as "the Minsk-born Pat Rishin (champion of Underhill and Wilson, S.C.)" is a play on the word "patrician." Darkbloom further explains: "That epithet [refers] to a popular critic, a would-be expert on Russian as spoken in Minsk and elsewhere." "Underhill" is a play on Norman Podhoretz's name; *pod gore* = "under hill," approximately. Podhoretz wrote a famous 1958 essay on Wilson, "The Last Patrician." In their post-*Onegin* ping-pong in *The New York Review*, Wilson accused Nabokov of adopting the Belarusian (Minsk) pronunciation of the word "czar."

WHY NABOKOV PURSUED his personal attacks is a mystery. The two men's fortunes had diverged, considerably. The second half of the 1960s was not particularly generous to Wilson, especially by contrast with Nabokov, upon whom fortune continued to smile.

Wilson's health had been poor for much of the decade. He had been suffering from gout, exacerbated by too much drinking, since the 1950s. He also developed serious heart problems, diagnosed as angina in the winter of 1961. There were many times during his later years when he had trouble walking, or ended up in a hospital, from which he more than once checked himself out. Getting to sleep was a problem, often resolved by scotch and Nembutal. His deteriorating health hardly interfered with his literary output, however. He reissued several books in the second half of the decade and composed some new ones as well: *A Prelude: Characters and Conversations from the Early Years of My Life*, taken from his journals, and *The Dead Sea Scrolls: 1947–1969*, a sequel to his successful 1955 journalism about the archaeological discoveries in Jordan's Qumran Caves.

Wilson experienced professional setbacks as well. He could fulminate all he wanted against U.S. imperialism and the taxmen in

his 1963 pamphlet, *The Cold War and the Income Tax: A Protest,*
but the IRS was demanding its $70,000 in unpaid taxes.* His wife,
Elena, appealed to family friend and Kennedy White House aide
Arthur Schlesinger, Jr., who jawboned the IRS into a $25,000 set-
tlement. That applied to back taxes only.[3] At one point during the
1960s, the service held a lien on all of Wilson's literary earnings.
He finally bounced the IRS sapajou off his back by auctioning off
his papers to Yale and by mortgaging his Talcottville, NY, home.

On the asset side of the ledger Wilson found himself on the
receiving end of several sizable, tax-free literary awards, including the one-thousand-dollar Emerson-Thoreau Medal from the
American Academy of Arts and Sciences. (He complained about
the ceremony in his journal, noting that "the dinner and drinks
were skimpy, as they are likely to be in Boston.") He also won the
National Book Committee's five-thousand-dollar National Medal
for Literature, and the munificent thirty-thousand-dollar Aspen
Award from the Great Books–loving grandees of the Aspen Institute. Wilson's doctor said his heart couldn't withstand a trip to
Aspen (elevation 7,900 feet), so instead he suffered through a lav-
ish banquet laid on in his honor at Manhattan's Waldorf-Astoria
Hotel.

Most of the attendees were rich Aspen Institute supporters. Jeffrey Meyers reports that "the oil millionaires who gave the award
did not know why he had won it and circulated *Who's Who* under
the table to find out who he was."[4] A plutocrat's wife asked if he
had written *Finlandia.* "The whole thing was slightly humiliat-
ing," Wilson recalled.[5] And not just for Wilson. His friend Paul
Horgan remembered that Wilson "leaped for the check, crying

---

* There are many examples of unintentional hilarity in Wilson's *The Income Tax,*
including the moment when the purportedly bereft Wilson admits to IRS inspectors
that he owns two homes and rents a third.

out, 'Tax-free! Tax-free!'" Wilson then insulted his benefactor, the Aspen president William Stevenson, by asking him to spell his name for a book inscription.[6]

The award was discontinued soon afterward. Wilson was the last person to win it.

In his journal *The Sixties*, published twenty years after his death, Wilson confessed that he was "a man of the twenties." The sixties weren't his decade. Paris wasn't the same; the Princeton Club had been remodeled, not much to his liking. Nylon stockings, "which used to last for months, now run at the slightest contact," and don't get him started on disposable razor blades.[7] His frenemy Alfred Kazin wrote of Wilson in the sixties that "he was so definitely not of this time." Kazin called the paunchy Wilson, brandishing a gold-topped walking cane, meandering up and down "the intellectuals' beach" in Wellfleet, a "character," and not a very appealing one:

> The sight of him in his Panama hat and well-filled Bermuda shorts, the cane propped up in the sand like a sword in a declaration of war, instantly brought out in me the mingled anxiety and laughter that I used to feel watching Laurel and Hardy crossing a precipice. There was so much mischief, disdain and intellectual solemnity wrapped up behind that getup, that high painfully distinct voice, that lonely proud face.[8]

The journals record a life of pain, fraught with world-weariness. "Reading the newspapers, and even the world's literature, I find that I more and more feel a boredom with and scorn for the human race," he wrote in 1966. That same year he drafted a poem, published in his 1971 memoir, *Upstate*: ". . . In a cage/I stalk from room to room, lose heat and speed./Now entering the dark defile of age."

He was seventy-one years old.

Across the ocean, amid the towering Alps, Vladimir Nabokov found the late 1960s very much to his liking. *Lolita* had made him a rich man who could travel where he wished and write exactly what he wanted. Nabokov did not need to go to the world; the world came to Nabokov. Whether it was a squad of *Time* magazine factotums converging on Montreux to prepare their unctuously flattering cover story ("Prospero's Progress") in May 1969, or the "hot" young Paramount producer Robert Evans come to read Nabokov's latest novel, *Ada*, in galleys, Nabokov luxuriated at the center of his self-created and self-contented universe. He busied himself by translating his "Sirin" stories from Russian into English (*Nabokov's Quartet*), with a new edition of *Speak, Memory*, and of course with the publication of the instant best seller *Ada, or Ardor: A Family Chronicle*. The book sold well on the strength of the author's worldwide fame, but many readers shared Evans's assessment of the book, which he speed-read twice, jet-lagged and high on amphetamines: "It was torture."

The world had confirmed what Nabokov and his wife had always suspected: that he was a genius. Immodest slips had always been part of the Nabokov show. In the 1950s he had started to refer to Anton Chekhov as "my predecessor." When he was translating the folklore tale *The Song of Igor's Campaign* in 1959, he wrote to Wilson that "Russia will never be able to repay all her debts to me."[9] "I think like a genius," was the provocative opening line to *Strong Opinions*, a collection of his interviews and essays. Brian Boyd correctly observes that "he thought the critical acclaim merely his belated and inevitable due."[10]

The *Time* cover story allowed him to dump on his fellow "American" authors. Philip Roth? "Farcical." Norman Mailer? "I detest everything that he stands for." He had joined Roth, Graham Greene, Jorge Luis Borges, and W. H. Auden as perennial Nobel Prize also-rans, writers whose names floated to the surface among each year's contenders, only to sink back again into the dispiriting slough of success and fame. Nineteen-seventy was again such a year, so that when a Montreux Palace Hotel clerk put through a long-distance call from Stockholm, the maestro braced himself for good news from the selection committee. Alas, it was only a graduate student asking for help with her thesis.*

In one of his most complicated literary démarches, Nabokov wrote a poem in 1959 parodying Boris Pasternak's famous lines about his accursed Nobel Prize. (Pasternak: "What wicked thing have I done . . . I, who forced the whole world to cry/Over my beautiful land." Nabokov: "What is the evil deed I have committed? . . . who set the entire world a-dreaming of my poor little girl?") But the venture is more complicated. In the final verse Nabokov speculates that, despite being banned in Russia, in a future day "a Russian branch's shadow shall be playing/upon the marble of my hand." In other words a future Russia would erect a statue to honor its loyal son Nabokov.

This speaks to one of his, and Pushkin's, private interests—the purported immortality of poets, as expressed in Horace's famous ode "Exegi Monumentum" ("I have raised a monument more permanent than bronze . . ."). Pushkin wrote an ode of the same name, which Nabokov, in one of the countless digressions in his *Onegin* "Commentary," called "one of the most subtle compo-

---

* Wilson had his own false Nobel moment. Late in life he eagerly tore open a thick envelope mailed from Stockholm, only to discover a crank letter alerting him to a world conspiracy of sex-changing assassins who communicated via ESP.

sitions in Russian literary history." Pushkin "slyly implies that only fools proclaim their immortality," Nabokov wrote. But a few years later, responding to what he regarded as Pasternak's wildly undeserved Nobel award, Nabokov suggested that it was he, not Pasternak, who would be memorialized in the Russian literary future.

He proved to be right. Moscow has been trying for years to raise money for a proper Pasternak monument, but St. Petersburg has already honored its native son. In 2007 St. Petersburg University unveiled a sculpture depicting the young, pensive Vladimir Nabokov in the courtyard of its Languages Department. There is one quotation engraved in the bronze, the famous final sentences of *The Gift:* a perfectly scanned, rhyming *Onegin* stanza.

Nabokov's politics, always sui generis, started to wax extreme. In 1965 he was one of President Lyndon Johnson's few staunch supporters among the literary set. WISHING YOU A PERFECT RECOVERY AND A SPEEDY RETURN TO THE ADMIRABLE WORK YOU ARE DOING was the text of a telegram he sent to the White House after Johnson's well-publicized appendectomy. "Vladimir was very pro-Vietnam," Jason Epstein recalled. "He thought the war in Vietnam was his way back to St. Petersburg. He had this fantasy of getting back home."

A few years later Vera wrote to a friend: "We are all for Nixon, emphatically against McGovern whom we find an irresponsible demagogue who deliberately misleads his followers and is doing damage to America."[11] (In the last month of his life Edmund Wilson proudly sported a George McGovern for President button.[12])

Around that time Nabokov sent a check to the Israeli ambassador in Switzerland during what became known as the Yom Kippur War: "I would like to make a small contribution to Israel's defense against the Arabolshevist aggression."

It was impossible not to notice Nabokov's ascension, high above the clouds. "Have you seen Volodya Nabokov on the cover of *Newsweek*?" Wilson asked their common friend Sonya Grynberg, mixing up his newsweeklies. "He looks like some model who had been hired to pose as Volodya Vladimir Nabokov."[13] Wilson's Russian was not so weak as to misstate his old friend's name, Vladimir Vladimirovich Nabokov. It must have been intended as a slight.

The Wilson feud was behind him, indeed the famous correspondence had been in abeyance for more than seven years, when Nabokov jotted off a quick "Dear Bunny" note in March 1971. He had heard from Elena Levin that Wilson had been ill. This was true; Wilson was beginning his precipitous decline and more often than not conducted his affairs from bed. (Pushkin, too, loved to work in bed, but that was because he was a sybarite who didn't feel like facing the day.) Nabokov said he had been rereading their correspondence, and felt again "the warmth of your many kindnesses, the various thrills of our friendship, that constant excitement of art and intellectual discovery. Please believe that I have long ceased to bear you a grudge for your incomprehensible incomprehension of Pushkin's and Nabokov's *Onegin*."

"Nabokov has suddenly written me a letter telling me that he values my friendship and that all has been forgiven," Wilson reported to Helen Muchnic: "He has been told that I have been ill, and it always makes him cheerful to think that his friends are in bad shape. He was mourning for Roman Grynberg at least ten years before he died."[14]

Wilson responded to Nabokov within the week, announcing that he was working on a collection of articles about Russia, which would include reworking his mammoth, anti-*Onegin* screed. He planned to correct a few of his own errors and cite "a few more of your ineptitudes." He added: "I have included an account of

my visit to you in Ithaca in a book that will be out this spring . . .
based on twenty years of Talcottville diary. I hope it will not again
impair our personal relations (it shouldn't)."

But of course it did.

Upstate: Records and Recollections of Northern New York,
published in the spring of 1971, was a surprise best seller, with
38,000 copies sold before the year was out. The 350-page-long
book detailed Wilson's fondness for his Talcottville neighbors, the
indigenous Iroquois as well as the colorful locals, some of whom
were his relatives on his mother's side, and many of whom were
close friends. Wilson devoted six pages of the book to the May
1957 visit to Vladimir and Vera Nabokov in Ithaca.

It was true, as Wilson wrote in his letter, that he had taken
a few pages from his journal recording the visit, and rewritten
them for publication in *Upstate.* But a glance at the journal, *The
Fifties,* shows that Wilson revised and expanded his impressions
of the Nabokovs for his 1971 audience.

For starters Wilson explained, in considerable detail, his long-
running "animated argument" with Nabokov about Russian and
English versification. "Volodya's insistent idea that Russian and
English verse are basically the same . . . is a part of his inheritance
from his father," Wilson wrote, already crossing several wires.
Nabokov did not think Russian and English prosody were "basically the same," and his "Notes on Prosody" nowhere makes that
claim. Any pseudopsychological allusion to his father was bound
to raise Nabokovian hackles.

Wilson intended to dig much deeper. He plowed up almost
every relic of their never-ending spat: how to pronounce "nihilist"; the real meaning of *fastidieux*; Nabokov's insistence that
writers like Turgenev (and, of course, Pushkin) didn't know much
English. "These false ideas," Wilson writes, "are prompted by his

compulsion to think of himself as the only writer in history who has been equally proficient in Russian, English and French, and he is always hopping people, with accents of outrage, for the pettiest kinds of mistakes."

It got worse. Wilson took a swing at Vera, to whom Nabokov was legendarily devoted. "Vera always sides with Volodya," he wrote, "and one seems to feel her bristling with hostility if . . . one argues with him." Wilson mentioned Vera's objections to his house gift, *L'Histoire d'O:* "She does not like my bringing him pornographic books. . . . She said with disgust that we had been giggling like schoolboys." Wilson then criticized Vera's hospitality, an unspeakable insult to a Russian, for whom all social relations proceed from a presumption of generosity to guests. Wilson's gout prevented him from sitting at the dinner table, so Vera had to bring him his food, separately. "I think it irked Vera a little to have to serve me thus."

"I always enjoy seeing them," Wilson wrote, then immediately retracted the thought:

> But I am always afterwards left with a somewhat uncomfortable impression. The element in his work that I find repellent is his addiction to *Schadenfreude.* Everybody is always being humiliated. . . .
>
> And yet he is in many ways an admirable person, a strong character, a terrific worker, Unwavering in his devotion to his family. . . . The miseries, horrors and handicaps that he has had to confront in his exile would have degraded or broken many, but these have been overcome by his fortitude and his talent.

Why did Wilson publish this diary excerpt, revised, extended, and more detailed in its criticism, if not to remind Nabokov of his previous, diminished existence as a disheveled academic ("his hair *ébouriffé* [tousled], consuming his little glasses of 'faculty' port and sherry") relegated to the Moosejaw of the Ivy League, that is, faraway Cornell in the Zemblan wilds of upstate New York? Where, Pnin-like, Nabokov was "overworked . . . with his academic duties and writing his books."

On the final night of this visit, Wilson noted that Nabokov had 150 papers to correct, prompting him to drink, and to reprise their many disagreements. Wilson also may have published this passage to remind Nabokov of Wilson's power, albeit fading power, in North American letters. Nabokov ruled Europe and the world, perhaps. But from the offices of *The New Yorker* off Times Square down to Publishers Row on Union Square, Wilson still commanded an audience.

A riposte was inevitable. Nabokov had seen *Upstate*, he informed *The New York Times Book Review:* "Since a number of statements therein wobble on the brink of libel, I must clear up some matters that might mislead trustful readers."

Let's be clear, Nabokov stated: Wilson "has no direct knowledge of my past. He has not even bothered to read my 'Speak, Memory.'" Wilson's idea that I inherited my ideas on prosody from my father "is too silly to refute. His muddleheaded and ill-informed description of Russian prosody only proves that he remains organically incapable of reading, let alone understanding, my work on the subject."

"Typical of his Philistine imagination," Nabokov wrote, "is his impression that at parties in our Ithaca house, my wife 'concentrated' on me and grudged 'special attention to anyone else.'"

"I am aware that my former friend is in ill health," he continued, explaining his letter as yielding to the demands of honor over compassion:

The publication of these "old diaries" (doctored, I hope, to fit the present requirements of what was then the future), in which living persons are but the performing poodles of the diarist's act, should be subject to a rule or law that would require some kind of formal consent from the victims of conjecture, ignorance, and invention.

The *Times* allowed Wilson a brief reply: "I anticipate some similar protests when he reads what I have written about him in my forthcoming volume on Russian subjects." He added: "I do not see that any question of 'honor' is involved in any of the matters he complains about. The only possible reply to his petulant outbursts is to repeat the comment of Degas to Whistler: 'You behave as if you had no talent.'"

This final exchange took place in November 1971. When Nabokov next took note of Edmund Wilson, it was to record his death.

Nabokov's tiny pocket diaries can be found at the New York Public Library. They are not really diaries, unlike Wilson's journal, which was very much a record of his current activities. These little notebooks are predictably unpredictable and eclectic. Months elapse with no entries, save Nabokov's annual reminder of Vera's birthday, or of their wedding anniversary. Sometimes he took note of weather patterns, and in the back, occasionally recorded his year-end bank balances. For instance, 1968 ended well: "Cash, . . . $6,500 Chase Man; Union de Banques Suisse fr. 26,000; (in Lolita acct) about $145,000."

Nabokov sometimes recorded dreams of note, including this one, on July 13, 1968: "Odd dream: Somebody on the stairs behind me takes me by the elbows. E.W. Jocular reconciliation."

There are only two entries for the week of June 12, 1972:

"Stopped [the heart drug] Segontin of which had taken some eighty pills since March 24," and "E.W. died."

WILSON KNEW the famous quote from Mark Twain's *Autobiography*, "I can speak more freely from the grave." Surely not by design—who isn't planning to live forever?—his harshest attack on Nabokov appeared in September 1972, three months after Wilson's death.

The little collection of essays, *A Window on Russia*, is quite sweet. It's more like a rearview-mirror window on Russia, written with great fondness by a visitor who will not be returning. Addressing his wife, Elena, in the introduction, Wilson mentions that he spent only five months in Russia, in 1935, and always struggled with the language. In the opening essay, reprised from his 1943 *Atlantic Monthly* article "Notes on Russian Literature," he writes, before throwing up his hands: "What, then, is one to do about Russian?"

The book also has a charming short piece, "A Little Museum of Russian Language." It is a funny little museum, displaying, among other things, the famous "little feet" from *Onegin*'s "Pedal Digression": "What exactly did Pushkin mean by the *damskiye nozhky* he so admired?" Wilson asked, and we ourselves still wonder. He has a Nabokov-like disquisition on twelve forms of the Russian verb *shchurit'*, which means dropping one's eyelids in a gesture of doubt, coquetry, or something else entirely. Wilson wins the hearts of generations of nonnative Russian students by listing three Russian words for "blizzard": *metel'*, *buran*, and *vy'uga*. "I do not understand the distinction, if any, between these words," he writes.

God bless you, Edmund. Neither do we.

Wilson included his famous *New York Review* attack on *Onegin* in *Window* ("My own attempts to tease Nabokov were not recognized as such but received in a virulent spirit") and attached a six-and-a-half-page coda to the article. This is Wilson's long-promised essay on Nabokov's fiction, first discussed in their letters a quarter century before. One of the many tensions in their relationship was Wilson's general refusal to write about, and thus promote, Nabokov's work. In 1944 Wilson did write a carefully worded and generally positive review of Nabokov's book on Nikolai Gogol, for *The New Yorker*. And in 1965, he wrote the *Onegin* article. Elena Levin, who knew both men very well, thought Nabokov was expecting some favorable publicity from Wilson during the lean, pre-*Lolita* years.[15] That may be so, but it is indisputable that Wilson was offering Nabokov considerable behind-the-scenes help with *The New Yorker* and with the big publishing houses.

Now, here it was: a brief—because Wilson was failing—but comprehensive overview of Nabokov's work, with some biographical observations tossed in. First, Wilson said he had read the "Sirin" work, for example, *Mary; The Luzhin Defense; King, Queen, Knave;* and *Invitation to a Beheading*, most of which Nabokov had translated into English; "I have found them rather disappointing," he reports. His primary complaint is that nothing really happens in these books: "Mr. Nabokov . . . regards a novel as a kind of game with the reader. By deceiving the latter's expectation, the novelist wins the game. But the device exploited in these novels is simply not to have anything exciting take place, to have the action peter out."

The short essay recycles some previous insults, calling Nabokov a man "who enjoy[s] malicious teasing and embarrassing practical jokes," and again cites "the addiction to *Schadenfreude* which pervades all his work." Wilson seems to be trying to praise *Lolita*, which he professed not to like when Nabokov had wanted him to like it. "His panorama of middle-class homes and motels is more amusing than his dreary and prosaic German vistas," Wilson says. "There is also something here like emotion—the ordeals of a torn personality."

Wilson likes to explain Nabokov by appealing to his unusual biography, as the brilliant Anglophile son of a well-to-do Anglophile, liberal politician in czarist Russia. This is fingernail-scraping-on-the-blackboard for Nabokov; Wilson insisted on calling Nabokov senior a "liberal," in quotes, which isn't exactly a compliment coming from the self-styled progressives of the "intellectuals' beach" of Wellfleet, Massachusetts. Wilson goes on to say that Nabokov "despises the Communist regime, and, it seems to me, does not even understand how it works or how it came to be. His knowledge of Russia, in fact, is very special, extremely limited."

Written by a man who bungled his way through five months in Russia, praising Lenin's dead, waxen "beautiful face, of exquisite fineness," this is crazy talk. Of course Nabokov hated the regime that, given the chance, would have executed his father, that had raked his departing passenger ship with machine-gun fire, that confiscated his family's fortune and more hurtfully the emotional property he celebrated in *Speak, Memory*. This is one essay of Wilson's to which Nabokov never responded, for obvious reasons.*

---

* In a way he did respond, albeit not publicly. Harvard's Houghton Library purchased Nabokov's personal copy of *A Window on Russia* in 2009. Nabokov marked up his books in his delicate, faint cursive, and he marked this one up quite thoroughly. Nabokov is a fastidious—in the English meaning, not the French—copyeditor, and he catches Wilson in dozens of small Russian errors. For example, it's *Novoye Vremya* (neuter) not *Novaya Vremya* (feminine); Belinsky's patronymic is Grigorievich, not Gregorivich, and so on. He even scores Wilson for misspelling the Gerund Heard

Wilson was gone but not forgotten in the Nabokov household. Vladimir had started to work on a second, revised edition of the *Onegin* project, to be published in a two-volume Princeton University Press paperback. Nabokov had gloated that take two would be exponentially more alienating to his critics, "even more gloriously and monstrously literal than the first." Nabokov felt that his first edition was "still not close enough and not ugly enough. In future editions I plan to defowlerize it still more drastically. I think I shall turn it entirely into utilitarian prose, with a still bumpier brand of English, rebarbative barricades of square brackets and tattered banners of reprobate words, in order to eliminate the last vestiges of bourgeois poesy and concession to rhythm."*

He had one chief critic in mind. He urged Princeton to speed up publication: "I would like to see my edition printed before confronting an irate Pushkin and a grinning E. Wilson beyond the cypress curtain."

Round the World, pochuya, the sniffing of the naggy, which Wilson spells "pochua." Naturally the man who insists on calling the Tolstoy novel "Anna Karenin" will not stand for Wilson's reference to "Alexandrina Tolstoya." He thinks Wilson's observations on vocabulary are inane, especially the contention that the Russian words for "snow" and "hole in the ice" are synonyms; "two different things," Nabokov corrects.

As for Wilson's comments on his novels and on his personality, Nabokov finds them hard to take. He underlines and double-question marks Wilson's contention that he "somewhere refers to himself as an Englishman." Nabokov doesn't like being compared to the "platform poetics" of Vladimir Mayakovsky and Yevgeny Yevtushenko, and he's pretty sure that Wilson misunderstood the ending of *Luzhin*. Nabokov likewise questions Wilson's assertion that "there is often a very young girl with whom, as in the case of *Lolita*, [the hero] is very much in love" in the early novels. One can only imagine the thundering letter he would have mailed to *The Guardian*, following Martin Amis's 2009 essay, "The Problem with Nabokov," which stated that six Nabokov novels "unignorably [concerned themselves] with the sexual despoliation of very young girls."

* These 1966 remarks in *Encounter* terrified Nabokov's editors at Bollingen, who fretted that they might have to replate all of *Onegin*, at tremendous expense. "We may prepare ourselves for his wanting to replace the translation with another," editor McGuire wrote to his boss, John Barrett, that year. "While this threatens to be a dreadful nuisance and expense, a revised text by Nabokov will surely be interesting and important."

During the early 1970s, Nabokov was wrestling with his authorized biographer, Andrew Field, for control of Field's book, *Nabokov: His Life in Part*. Initially Nabokov's bibliographer, Field, a brainy, Harvard-trained, quasi-Nabokovian junior academic, signed on to write about Nabokov at the end of the writer's life. The whole project veered sideways, badly, with legal threats and accusations of bad faith flying in all directions. Field eventually wrote three books about Nabokov, each of them a bit discursive, digressive, and showily erudite—that is, Nabokovian to the core.

The Nabokov-Field dispute merits a book of its own. Nabokov hated the Boswellian grit of literary biographies, "the human interest chitchat," and regretted sharing dozens of casual anecdotes with Field. He despised almost everything about the draft manuscript of *Nabokov: His Life in Part*, but he especially disliked Field's treatment of the contretemps with Wilson.

Field began his account of the Wilson-Nabokov relationship with an anecdote from 1944. The story is innocent enough. Wilson wanted to take Nabokov's son Dmitri and Vladimir to a special doctor in Manhattan, but Wilson got the address wrong. Wilson and Nabokov were waiting for Dmitri, who had instead shown up at the correct address. Wilson was fuming about the chronically late, irresponsible Russians, but it was he who is in error. "He had taken *me* to the wrong house!" Nabokov crows. "Isn't that a marvelous story?"

This "trivial incident," Field wrote, may have been the only time "when a clear advantage of one man over the other was acknowledged by both men on *anything*."[16]

Change it, Nabokov demanded. He wanted the incident described as "the first but not the last time that an unquestionable advantage was won by Nabokov over Wilson in the course of a two-decade-long friendship." In a side note to Field, Nabokov explained, "I'm afraid I cannot authorize any doubts anent your subject's clearly winning the *Battle of EO*." The original language made it into the book.

One paragraph later Field called the men "competitors." "We were never competitors," Nabokov notes. "In what, good gracious?" "Competitors" stayed.

Detailing Wilson's solicitude for Nabokov, Field wrote that "Wilson was so energetic in Nabokov's interest that he even turned to friends with requests for loans." "Impossible," Nabokov objected. This, too, stayed in the text.

In his draft Field mentioned that Nabokov and Wilson worked together translating *The Song of Igor's Campaign*. Nabokov objected, apparently forgetting that the two men discussed an article on *Igor* for *The New Yorker* in 1948, which Nabokov eventually wrote, and the magazine rejected.[17] In the heady post-*Lolita* years, when almost anything with Nabokov's name found a publisher, Random House issued his translation of and commentary on *Igor*—actually a retranslation; he had created a version for his Cornell lectures—done without any input from Wilson.

But in rebutting Field's minor inaccuracy, Nabokov asserted: "We never worked together," which was untrue. One of his first bylines in an American magazine was his translation of Pushkin's "little tragedy," *Mozart and Salieri*, for the *New Republic*, a collaboration with Wilson. The two men exchanged draft outlines of a proposed joint book on Russian literature for several years.

Most egregiously Nabokov attempted to recast the well-known story of how the two men met. In the version Nabokov wanted Field to print, "Nabokov's first awareness of Wilson's existence was in the late summer of 1940 when N. [*sic*] received in Vermont a letter from him suggesting they meet in New York. They did." This completely reverses the terms of trade, as if Wilson sought out the great novelist in his summer retreat. The truth of the matter was that Nabokov's well-established relative, the composer Nicolas Nabokov, begged Wilson to lend a hand to his needy cousin, and Wilson graciously complied.

Longevity has its privileges—in this case, rewriting history not as it was, but as one wishes it had been.

Just Kidding?

When the *Onegin* imbroglio was at its height, the editors of *The New York Review of Books* sent Wilson copies of the feud-related letters they intended to publish. A letter from Stephen P. Jones of Noank, Connecticut, appeared in the *Review*, in edited form. Wilson kept a copy of the complete version in his files. Jones professed to admire both combatants, and treated himself to a hearty lunch before tackling Wilson's meaty critique:

> It was upon a full stomach then, that I realized that the whole article was a hoax and that Mr. Wilson had no hand in it whatsoever, that it had been written by Mr. Nabokov as an appendix to Pale Fire and given to Mr. Wilson as a gesture of the friendship referred to in Mr. Wilson's first paragraph in order that he might buy his dog one of those decadently delightful cushions.

Jones was a real fan. The dog cushion made a Checkers-like appearance in *The Cold War and the Income Tax*, Wilson's rant against the Internal Revenue Service. Wilson claimed an IRS

agent reprimanded him "for having spent too much money on
liquor . . . and for having bought a $6 mat for my dog."[1]

The *Review* deleted the dog reference, and also Jones's helpful
proposal for resolving the nastiness between the two men:

> As to whether or not horses 'sniff ' snow or 'sense' it or merely
> 'smell' it, I think we should do what we always do here in town
> when two old men at the hotel fight over the bathroom: have
> the chambermaid swallow the key. But yet again, we are very
> provincial here with long winter nights, nasal horses, deep
> drifts, etc.

Jones anticipated by a few months the outraged Robert Lowell's suggestion in *Encounter* that Nabokov was spoofing his readers with his nine hundred-plus pages of *Onegin* arcana. Also in
Encounter, Paul Fussell detected a whiff of parody in Nabokov's
"Notes on Prosody": "He has always delighted in parody, and
what we have here is like the parody of a dissertation or a text-
book." It escaped no one's notice that just two years earlier Nabokov had published *Pale Fire*, a sinister and complicated parody of
a "novel in verse" accompanied by a ridiculously overdetermined
commentary.

The idea that Nabokov was playing games with his audience
in constructing *Onegin*'s Rube Goldberg–like scholarly apparatus
seems ridiculous, and the notion that Nabokov the sleight-of-hand
artist may have been feigning umbrage during his feud with Wilson seems equally preposterous. It wouldn't be worth mentioning,
except that the elderly Wilson apparently believed it to be true.

Nabokov was arguably the twentieth century's Trickster King,
addicted to punning, a form of humor which Wilson hated, and

to games of all kinds, especially hoaxes.* In his Cornell literature lectures, which he read from a prepared text, he would sometimes start reading again *da capo*, and wait for the drowsy undergrads to figure out what had happened. He once included "Sirin," his Russian pen name, in a list of the five greatest Russian poets. When a student asked who that was, Nabokov answered, "Ah, I shall read from his work," but didn't elaborate.[2]

Harry Levin remembered a Cambridge gathering in the early 1940s, when the freshly arrived Nabokov convinced a prominent, left-leaning academic that Joseph Stalin wasn't the real dictator of the Soviet Union. Pointing to a photograph from the Tehran summit, Nabokov put his finger on Pavlovsky, Stalin's ubiquitous interpreter. There—that's the man who's really running the country, Nabokov insisted. Stalin is just the front man.[3]

Nabokov thought liberal academics: (1) knew nothing about the USSR; and (2) would believe anything, Q.E.D.

One of Nabokov's most elaborate tricks proved to be a hoax within a hoax, a gloss of Churchill's famous description of the Soviet Union, "a riddle wrapped in a mystery inside an enigma." In 1950, he wrote an unpublished "Chapter Sixteen" to his childhood memoir *Conclusive Evidence*, which, reedited and renamed, would later become the classic *Speak, Memory*. Chapter 16 was a parody of a joint book review, of *Conclusive Evidence* and of *When Lilacs Last*, a fictional, patrician New England memoir (a "beautiful, compassionate, intensely feminine quest in the king-

---

* Don't forget acrostics. Nabokov sent a lengthy letter to his friend *The New Yorker* editor Katharine White, berating her for rejecting his short story "The Vane Sisters." "I feel that the New Yorker has not understood 'The Vane Sisters' at all," he wrote. "Let me explain a few things." The last paragraph, he said, "for a more attentive reader contains the additional delight of a solved acrostic," formed by the capital letters at the beginning of each sentence. White replied, in so many words, that *The New Yorker* wasn't *Puzzle Week:* "We did not work out your acrostic, to be sure, that being rather out of the *New Yorker*'s line."

dom of things past"), which the author proceeded to ignore. The "review" was jocoserious, on the one hand mocking the flowery pieties of American book reviewing of the time:

> the diamond-pattern of art and the muscles of sinuous memory are combined in one strong and supple movement and produce a style that seems to slip through grass and flowers toward the warm flat stone upon which it will richly coil.[4]

At the same time the "review" was pregnant with insights into the ambitious, little-known Russian-American writer. Nabokov discussed at some length his pre-American career as Sirin, who "had gained a lasting place in Russian literature, despite the fact that his books were banned in his mother country." In passing he explained how his transition to writing in English trumped the experience of Joseph Conrad, "whose English style, anyway, was a collection of glorified clichés."

Writing in the voice of an anonymous reviewer, Nabokov said he lived "in the simple disguise of an obscure college professor of literature with spacious vacations devoted to butterfly hunting in the West." Our reviewer knew the author's shortcomings: "One cannot help being irritated by certain peculiarities of Nabokov's manner . . . [which] seems to combine a good deal of absentmindedness with his pedantism." The man *is* annoying! "Few people will share his contention that [T. S.] Eliot's poetry is essentially platitudinous," we read. "Then, too, there is his contempt for Dostoevsky which makes Russians shudder and is disapproved of in the academic circles of our greatest universities."

But inside this hoax Nabokov discussed one of his most famous hoaxes, then known to a relatively small group of Russian émigré literati. A prominent critic of the Russian diaspora, George

Adamovich, admired Sirin's prose but refused to like his poetry. As an obituary tribute to a famous Russian poet, Vladislav Khodasevich, Nabokov published an eloquent verse eulogy, in the name of "Vasily Shishkov." Adamovich could not contain his elation: "Who is Vasily Shishkov?" he wrote. "Every line, every word is talented." In the Paris journal *Posledniye Novosty* (*Latest News*), Adamovich quoted all the Shishkov he could, and repeated: "Again I must ask who is this Vasily Shishkov?"[5] Nabokov soon revealed all in an obviously fictional short story that purported to be an "interview" between Sirin and the mysterious Shishkov,* who conveniently disappeared to work on his new magazine, *A Survey of Pain and Vulgarity*.

That was in 1939. The latter-day Nabokov, living large on Lake Geneva, never lost his taste for trickery. To prove a point—just what point isn't clear—he insisted in 1967 that the *Saturday Evening Post* publish a letter in which he accused the magazine of libeling a Cornell colleague, "the poet Sam Fortuni." He admitted that Fortuni was (1) fictional and (2) an anagram, but he wanted to punish the *Post* for departing from the verbatim text of an interview he had agreed to publish. The hapless *Post* editor complained that (1) no one could decipher the anagram and (2) printing a letter of apology for defaming someone who didn't exist seemed a bit much, frankly. Nabokov reiterated his demand, and helpfully explained the mathematical anagram, a "very simple combina-

---

* Shishkov was not a name chosen at random. Nabokov's biographer Brian Boyd thinks the root *shishka* (pinecone), echoes the equally famous fake poet Alexander Travnikov (*trava* means "grass"), invented by Khodasevich himself. Boyd further notes that Shishkov was the maiden name of Nabokov's great-grandmother. I wonder if Nabokov wasn't invoking Adm. Alexander Shishkov, the right-wing poetaster who became Czar Nicholas I's literary censor. Shishkov disliked Pushkin, but nonetheless approved publication of chapter 1 of *Eugene Onegin*, recognizing its brilliance. Pushkin directs an aside to Shishkov in *Onegin*, 8:14, prompting a lengthy explanation in Nabokov's Commentary.

tion SAM FORTUNI = 12345678910 = 35178942106 = MOST UNFAIR (a phrase actually used in my letter)." The letter ran.

Was Nabokov gaming Wilson during their famous feud? The *New Statesman* poured gasoline on this fire by publishing a 1967 review of Andrew Field's book, *Nabokov: His Life in Art*. In 1967 Field and Nabokov were still close, and Alan Brien, reviewing for the *Statesman*, suggested that the book was written by Nabokov himself. Brien asked if "this, like its predecessor, *Pale Fire*, is an elaborate literary hoax with only a glancing surface resemblance to a serious critical study by another author?" "We dedicated Nabokovians" know the master's love of pseudonyms, of which "Andrew Field" may well be one, he argued. In jest. We think.

Wilson saved this review, and the odd letters that the *Statesman* published afterward. One correspondent, Ronald Vincent-Smith, agreed that the Field book gave "off a strong smell of *Pale Fire*." The following week, one A. Bluhm implored the *Statesman:* "Will you pu-lease stop kidding (Hi, Lolita) and publish an authoritative editorial statement about the bona fides of Andrew Field, alias Vivian Darkbloom . . ." For the record, Andrew Field was and is a real person, and, as previously noted, Vivian Darkbloom is a fictional anagram of Vladimir Nabokov that he used in both *Lolita* and *Pale Fire*.[6]

This bizarre exchange gave Wilson a very bad idea. The University of Missouri professor Gennady Barabtarlo was the first to spot the rough draft of a letter to the *Statesman* among Wilson's papers. Wilson, Barabtarlo thought, was in a tight spot: "Wilson must have found his position thoroughly uncomfortable because of the swarm of blunders and indefensible stances in his original article that Nabokov had exposed, and was bewildered by all this gallimaufry in print and afraid that he might have missed some disguised digs of Nabokov's cunning."[7]

So Wilson drafted a pseudonymous letter to the *Statesman,* instructing his secretary not to type it on his personal stationery because "it is part of a joke." Although not entirely legible, here is what the handwritten draft says:

> . . . the recent polemics between Nabokov and Edmund Wilson have [illegible] elements of hoax. My theory would be that a comedy had been planned by Nabokov and Wilson.
>
> The original article in The New York Review of Books on Nabokov's edition of "Evgeni Onegin" was authentically the work of Wilson, who intentionally included in it a few rudimentary mistakes in Russian. He then toyed [?] a retort by Nabokov in which *he caricatures the virulence with which that brilliant writer is in the habit of attacking anyone who has aroused his animosity by criticizing him or competing with him.* [Emphasis added]

The withering ripostes and counterthrusts, Wilson wrote, were actually written inversely, with Nabokov playing the part of Wilson, and so on. "This . . . shows with clarity just how badly smarting were the cuts Wilson had sustained in the clash," Barabtarlo elaborated. Quite wisely, Wilson never sent the letter.

Barabtarlo unearthed another oddity in the Wilson papers, a letter of support from an unidentifiable Russian correspondent. Here is Barabtarlo's translation:

> . . . I congratulate you from the bottom of my heart. I do so because, in the first place, you so aptly, so brilliantly, so profoundly, and so caustically let that mister have it whom we both hold in rather low esteem and whom moreover I for one

(as a Russian), do not quite take for a writer, although I like his Eugene Onegin very much. . . .

You are the only writer who could accomplish that tour de force and that's why it seems to me that you are the only person in the world who could, and in my opinion should translate Eugene Onegin into English for mankind, for Pushkin, and maybe for yourself. You hold all the aces in your hand: you are an Anglo-Saxon, a famous and profound writer, you know thoroughly the Russian language, without commanding it (because you rarely speak it) and, besides, nobody feels and loves that period of Russian revolutionary life quite as you do.

Barabtarlo notes "the extraordinarily striking resemblance this letter bears to the style of the Double in Nabokov's short story 'Double Talk'!" In other words the letter may have been a crude hoax mailed to Wilson by Nabokov.

This theme would emerge one last time before Wilson's death, in the pages of *The New York Times Book Review*. The *Times* had reviewed *Upstate*, Wilson's memoir of his times spent at his ancestral manse in Talcottville, New York. *Upstate*, published in 1971, included the previously cited barbed account of Wilson's 1957 visit to the Nabokovs in Ithaca.

The *Times* published two letters in response to its review, both from men who claimed to have been at Cornell at the time. The correspondent Diron Frieders (an anagram for "Sordid Refiner"; sorry, I couldn't resist) said he was "an objective observer [who felt] compelled to step into the fray." Frieders claimed to have been a student of Nabokov's who had gathered "some rather precise data about the 'friendship' of these two friendly enemies."

The two men's hostility stemmed from two incidents, accord-

ing to Frieders. First he recounted that when Nabokov initially
tried to contact Wilson in 1940, the celebrated critic kissed off
the émigré nobody with one of his famous, preprinted "Edmund
Wilson Regrets" cards. (No fan or foe of Wilson's has ever suggested this to be true.) Frieders also wrote that, while a guest at
the Nabokovs' in 1958,

> Wilson (according to my sources) shoved his foot into one of
> Vladimir's cherished butterfly nets, ripping it beyond repair. . . .
> N, to this day, is convinced that the incident was no accident but
> rather a demonstration of contempt for his much-publicized
> hobby. (Wilson at one time had commented that "Butterfly-
> chasing is an activity unbecoming to a writer.")[8]

This likewise seems to be a crazy fabrication of the kind of colorful anecdote that would quickly have entered the annals of the
two men's enmity, if true.

Frieders had more to say. He challenged Wilson's statement
that he found "Nabokov's addiction to *Schadenfreude* repellent,"
adding:

> . . . This statement *does* cry out for comment. Being fully
> aware of Vladimir's almost obsessive contempt for the theo-
> ries of Freud, Wilson habitually twisted the meaning of this
> word to create the impression that it meant 'hatred of Freud,' an
> implication that never failed to make Nabokov squirm. Thus,
> Wilson was occasionally guilty of *Schadenfreude* himself.

A second correspondent, Mark Hamburg, also served up the
story of the torn butterfly net. Hamburg said he visited the Nabo-

kov home as a graduate student, and found professor "Morris Bishop standing in the hallway with Nabokov—while the latter showed him a butterfly net with its bottom ripped out." He elaborated:

"Surely you can't suspect Wilson of this merely because you met the wrong train," said Bishop.

Nabokov, obviously upset, answered, "We have had serious differences of opinion on Russian prosody. . . . His condition makes him quite non-ambulatory. . . . Still, he brought a pair of nail scissors. I cannot be certain."

Writing from Naples, Florida, just a few months before his death, Wilson told the *Times* that there was "not one word of truth" in the Frieders and Hamburg letters.

I don't think I ever spoke of *Schadenfreude* in his presence and certainly never thought it had anything to do with Freud.

I don't remember ever seeing his butterfly nets and never disapproved of his lepidopteral activities. On the contrary, I liked to hear him talk about them.

There could have been no question of his meeting the wrong train when I visited him in Ithaca, because I came in a car.

I suspect that both these letters were written by Nabokov himself, who may find that he is sometimes at a loss to amuse himself in Montreux.[9]

And we are off to the races again: "Puzzled queries from correspondents oblige me to react," Nabokov wrote to the newspaper, "with some delay, to the tasteless parody (posing as letters in this space) from 'Diron Frieders' and 'Mark Hamburg,' which I take to be the phony names of one or two facetious undergraduates, judging by the style and piffle."

He asked the paper to "do a service to Edmund Wilson as well as to truth if you would point out that neither he nor I composed these letters."

No such assurance was forthcoming, but Mark Hamburg did write in to assure the *Book Review* that he very much existed: "Edmund Wilson—and now Vladimir Nabokov—are mistaken when they assume I do not exist." Hamburg said he used to be Morris Bishop's graduate assistant, and confirmed his bona fides by rattling off insider knowledge of the Cornell campus of the 1950s: "Jim's Place (the bar); the "Dutch"; Willard Straight; "Baldy" Wilson, the Donne scholar . . . and lastly, Campus Widow Grace Verezanno."[10]

"Of course I'm greatly flattered," Hamburg added, "that Wilson (an old hero) should think I wrote a letter he attributed to Nabokov (whom I revere)."

The *Book Review* editor appended a note to the Hamburg letter: "Thus ends our coverage. Or, as Caruso once remarked: '*La commedia è finita!*' "

Diron Frieders never surfaced again. Were Wilson's suspicions justified? Was he being played? Cornell has no record of either a Diron Frieders or a Mark Hamburg being on campus during the late 1950s. Perhaps we will never know. Nabokov was the unparalleled literary gamesman of his time, and as his biographer Brian Boyd once wrote: "Vladimir Nabokov was a game he played to the hilt."

11

Why?

Here is a scene from Andrew Field's *Nabokov: His Life in Part*, published just a few weeks before the novelist's death:

> Much of the public face of Nabokov consists of well-practiced bits of vignettes—when he spoke of Edmund Wilson, for example, he would weigh their friendship and then slowly decide that, in spite of all that has happened in recent years, he was a very old friend—**in certain ways my closest,** and having said that he tilts his head and looks at his wife in an owlish and arch manner. I myself witnessed this particular scene, and as his biographer of course I have on record another instance in which he enacted essentially the same scene for someone else.[1]

The boldface line is a direct quotation by another name. Nabokov had forbidden Field to quote from their exchanges. As the men's relations worsened, Nabokov suggested that Field's interview tapes were fabrications, so the amanuensis dreamed up this elaborate workaround. He printed direct quotations in boldface, but without quotation marks.

Here is a piece of theater: Nabokov tells a third party that
Edmund Wilson was "in certain ways" his closest friend. Then he
punctuates the ambiguous comment with a knowing look toward
Vera, his closest friend in all ways. In what ways *was* Wilson
Nabokov's closest friend? Because of shared childhood connec-
tions, Nabokov was doubtless closer, in certain ways, to Georgy
Hessen, a longtime family friend, and to Samuel Rosoff, a Tenishev School classmate ("a sensitive schoolmate of mine"—*Speak,
Memory*) with whom he reestablished contact in Switzerland. He
was extremely close to his sister Elena Sikorski, who spent the
second half of her life in Geneva, and often shared vacations with
Vladimir and Vera. The couple took care of their lifelong friend
Anna Feigin, Vera's cousin, who had helped them with loans
and hospitality during the lean years in Europe. These were life
friendships, of shared time and experience.

Many of us still have best friends from childhood whom we
may see once or twice a decade, yet they remain best friends. Wilson and Nabokov were not like that. Their friendship fed on the
oxygen of intellectual discourse. When Nabokov writes to tell
Wilson that he misses him, he misses the vigorous repartee that
is only partly captured in the written exchanges. For many years
they had their lives' works in common, and in certain ways—
certainly when it came to talking about literature and writing—
yes, Wilson was Nabokov's best friend.

So how does a friendship pass from genuine intimacy to loathing? From the borrowing of socks to the rewriting of personal
histories? Samuel Johnson remarked that "one of the duties of
friendship [is] to hear complaints with patience, even when complaints are vain." In the voluminous Wilson-Nabokov correspondence, one finds a two-thousand-word-long, June 1944 letter from
Nabokov that includes a graphic account of bleeding diarrhea

brought on by food poisoning. Assigned to a Cambridge hospital room with "an old man dying from acute cardiac trouble," Nabokov monitored his bunkmate's end-stage ravings and shared them with Wilson: "all very interesting and useful to me."

For heaven's sake, Nabokov even *dreamed* of Wilson:

Am coming down steps of Lausanne-like railway station and meet Edmund. . . . He is about to catch a train. I tell him I'll go "upstairs" to see him off. He says: only Russians use "upstairs" in that sense. He walks briskly along the platform and I notice how fit he looks in a dark-grey suit. We lose each other in the crowd and the train glides away.[2]

How did we travel from "Dear Bunny," and "Dear Volodya," to Please Lose My Address and By the Way I'm Removing Your Blurbs from All My Books?

"A black cat came between us—Boris Pasternak's novel '*Doctor Zhivago*,' " is how Nabokov explained the rift in his "death interview" with Alden Whitman, the obituary writer for *The New York Times*. "He started the quarrel," Nabokov said, confident that either he or Wilson would be dead when his words appeared. (Wilson predeceased him by five years.) Whitman added that the bad relations were "exacerbated" when "Mr. Nabokov published his annotated English version of 'Eugene Onegin.' "[3]

I suppose Wilson did start the quarrel, by pillorying *Onegin* in *The New York Review*. But that was the violent tremor released by tectonic plates that had been rubbing against each other for many years. In a brief 1965 note to Barbara Epstein, Nabokov referred to Wilson's attack on the *Onegin* translation. "Though well aware of the real reason behind this attack," he wrote, "I consider this reason far too sad and private to be aired in print."[4]

The "real reason" hints at a dark revelation. But the truth seems more prosaic. It looks as if Wilson was suffering from a case of Nabokov fatigue manifesting itself as old-fashioned envy. In the course of a quarter century the two men's fortunes had dramatically reversed. When Nabokov came to America in 1940, he could only have been flattered to have Wilson as both audience and promoter. The country's leading literary critic is reviewing drafts of your stories and articles, correcting your grammar, and then passing them on to his influential friends? That's an enviable situation for anyone, much less a barely landed immigrant.

Yes, it was a two-way street, because Wilson feasted on the intellectual banquet of Nabokov's capacious knowledge of Russian and European literature. But over time it mattered less. Nabokov found his own, wider audience. Editors came to him; he didn't need an intermediary. Wilson, alternately indifferent to and fascinated by the tidal wave of Nabokov's post-*Lolita* fame, started to lose interest in the friendship. After all, Russian and Pushkin were just two of his many enthusiasms.

In 1991 Gennady Barabtarlo visited the Wilson archive at Yale's Beinecke Library and filed a dispatch in the online magazine *Cycnos*. Reading Wilson's notes and letters, Barabtarlo detected "an ulcerous trace of envy on Wilson's part that . . . became especially acute after *Lolita*—not because Wilson secretly admired it (he did not) but because he thought that Nabokov succeeded commercially where he, Wilson, had failed." The two men had switched places in the cultural firmament. "The novel and the Hollywood film [of *Lolita*] made Nabokov rich and a celebrity," Barabtarlo wrote, "while Wilson continued to work up nineteenth-century statesmen, generals and second-line writers, as well as to attack big-power imperialism."

The "statesmen, generals and second-line writers" describes the subject matter of Wilson's 1962 book, *Patriotic Gore*, which—in addition to likening Lincoln to Lenin—devoted considerable space to such lesser-known writers as George Washington Cable, John William De Forest, and Thomas Nelson Page. Wilson flexed his anti-imperialist muscles in *The Cold War and the Income Tax: A Protest*, and elsewhere.

Barabtarlo further notes that Nabokov "never misdeemed their relative worth as men of letters, but came to realize in full only too late that Wilson thought contrariwise, considering Nabokov as he did an ingenious, even brilliant but superficial and possibly imitative writer and negligible thinker." It's true that Wilson regarded himself as Nabokov's peer, or better, and that over time he lost patience with his friend's writing.

Wilson committed another sin: He claimed to understand what made Nabokov tick. Following his nervous breakdown in 1929, Wilson wrote *The Wound and the Bow*, explaining how trauma breeds artistic creativity. "He had come to the conclusion that he had discovered the secret source of Nabokov's art in *schaden-freude*," Brian Boyd writes. Wilson discerned a chilly soullessness in his former friend, an effect of the family's jarring emigration, and of the assassination of Nabokov's father.[5] But Nabokov declared himself to be unfathomable, and hated all psychologizing, especially when it focused on him and his work. He dismissed Wilson's analysis as "figments of his warped fancy."

It also became clear over time that the two men were very different writers. Wilson took literature seriously, sometimes too seriously. In his fiction his seriousness of purpose betrayed him. One would have welcomed some Nabokovian levity in *Hecate County*, for instance, but there was none. Yet Nabokov's "deep-lying inhumanity, or, more precisely, unhumanity"—the eminent critic George Steiner's phrase[6]—must have worn Wilson down.

He always believed that writing had a purpose, and many of his purposes testified to his sense of justice and his ever-inquiring mind. He publicized the downtrodden Harlan County coal miners in 1931 and campaigned for Native Americans' rights at least a decade before their plight gained national attention. *Patriotic Gore* reassessed the blithely accepted foundation myths of the Civil War. *The Scrolls from the Dead Sea*, his groundbreaking popularization of Old and New Testament apocrypha, anticipated the vast, protoacademic Jesus industry of the final quarter of the twentieth century.

Contrast these outings with Nabokov's declaration: "My books are blessed by a total lack of social significance."[7]

One of Wilson's unrealized ambitions was to create an American version of France's government-funded *Bibliothèque de la Pléiade*, an authoritative and accessible collection of classic literature. Wilson hated pedantry and despaired that his nemesis, the fusty Modern Language Association, would hijack his idea for a library of national classics, which they indeed tried to do. Wilson wanted excellent editions of great classics priced for mass consumption. A two-thousand-page, four-volume doorstop translation of *Eugene Onegin*, costing $150, would be a precise example of what Wilson did *not* want to see in bookstores.

Where Nabokov was concerned, Wilson appreciated the prose but not the poetry, figuratively speaking. He enjoyed *Speak, Memory* and portions of Nabokov's early work, such as *Sebastian Knight*. But he tired quickly of the gaming, the frippery, the language tricks, the difficult allusions. He seems not to have read the finished version of *Bend Sinister*, and he abandoned *Lolita* halfway through. He dismissed *Pale Fire* and *Ada* with a snap of his fingers. I find it hard to believe that he read those books, either.

Wilson was in excellent company. This is V. S. Naipaul speaking, but it could just as well be Wilson: "What is [Nabokov's] style? It's bogus, calling attention to itself. Americans do that. All those beautiful sentences. What are they for?"[8]

Wilson doubtless felt unfairly eclipsed by the international acclaim that enveloped Nabokov's post-*Lolita* endeavors, but Nabokov had been nursing his own slights. He expressed pique more than once that Wilson failed to finish some of his books, and that Wilson never used his clout to promote him in the early days. Elena Levin told Martha Duffy of *Time* that Nabokov had been hoping for some favorable reviews from Wilson, and she speculated to the biographer Brian Boyd that Wilson probably never published his promised overview of Nabokov's work because his Russian simply wasn't up to it.[9] Levin told Duffy in 1969 that "Wilson does not know enough Russian to write about Nabokov or Pushkin." Then how was he able to trash Nabokov's work on *Onegin?* "He simply recognized that this was not a good translation," Levin replied.[10]

IN A 1942 LETTER to Roman Grynberg, Nabokov addressed his relations with Wilson, whom he had known for only two years. "I love a violin in personal relationships, but in this case there is no way one can let out a heartfelt sigh or casually unburden a soft fresh bit of oneself," Nabokov wrote. "Still, there is a great deal else to make up for it."[11]

The Russian word for friend is *droug*, and it is a pregnant word indeed. Russian friendships almost rise to the status of blood brotherhood. It is quite possible that Nabokov always regarded Wilson as an American friend, with all the friability that that implies, and not a *nostoyashchy droug*—a "real friend"—the highest compliment a Russian can bestow.

What of Wilson? What kind of friend was he?

Fanatically loyal, one would have to conclude, especially to his Princeton classmates, whom he regarded as a literary band of brothers. The world has forgotten John Peale Bishop, but Wilson was promoting his classmate's poetry and prose throughout the latter's brief life, and lamented to anyone who would listen that Bishop's wealthy wife had perverted his friend's true calling: literature. Their classmate F. Scott Fitzgerald died even younger— Bishop lived to age fifty-two, Fitzgerald to forty-four—yet Wilson evinced a fidelity to Scott apparently unblemished by envy. In 1933 Wilson wrote to Fitzgerald: "I have just read Hemingway's new short stories . . . now is your time to creep up on him," repeating the last phrase twice.[12] Wilson edited Fitzgerald's posthumous novel, *The Last Tycoon*, for free and battled mightily with the authorized biographer Arthur Mizener on his late friend's behalf. "They [the Fitzgeralds] had a genius for imaginative improvisations of which they were never quite deprived even in their later misfortunes," was one of many corrective observations he sent to Mizener in 1950.[13]

Wilson showed tremendous loyalty even to friends who had jumped the rails. "In spite of our unusual loathing of one another's views, I'd very much like to see you," he wrote to the editor and poet Allen Tate in 1951.[14] Wilson and John Dos Passos had been friends since the 1920s, and Wilson twice intervened to question his old comrade's sanity. "What in God's name has happened to you?" Wilson exclaimed in 1938. "You've been plugging the damned Stalinist line, which gets more and more cockeyed by the minute.[15] Twenty-six years later he called out the slip-sliding Dos Passos yet again: "What on earth has happened to you? How can you take Goldwater seriously?"[16]

In *Sir Vidia's Shadow*, his book about his ruptured friendship with V. S. Naipaul, Paul Theroux observed that "friendship is plainer but deeper than love. A friend knows your faults and forgives them, but more than that, *a friend is a witness* [emphasis added.]"[17] I think Wilson became an inconvenient witness for Nabokov, a man who remembered the fervent supplications for help from Nicolas Nabokov ("Help, dear Edmund Edmundovich. Do whatever you can"), who remembered the years when Nabokov had to borrow money from Roman Grynberg to pay Dmitri's private school tuitions. Wilson had known Nabokov as a man in need, and continued their friendship into a time when Nabokov preferred to be regarded as a man who needed nothing from anyone.

In the end both men could live without each other. Nabokov had achieved autarky in the Swiss Alps, with all the comforts of not-home in the company of the few intimate acquaintances he cared about. Despite his best efforts to subvert it, Wilson had a stable marriage and also a dwindling but supportive public for his works.

After Wilson died, Vera Nabokova wrote a letter to his widow, Elena. "I would like to tell you how fond Vladimir has always been of Edmund despite the unfortunate turn in their relations. We always think of Edmund in terms of past friendship and affection; not of the so unnecessary hostilities of recent years." Two years later, when Elena Wilson was assembling the men's letters for publication, Vladimir wrote to her: "I need not tell you what agony it was rereading the exchanges belonging to the early radiant era of our correspondence."

12

As I Was Saying . . .

Even in the decade after the two writers' deaths, the *Onegin* translation controversy occasionally lurched out of its coffin. In 1977, the year that Nabokov died, the retired British diplomat Charles Johnston published his rhyming, metered translation that so enchanted the young writer Vikram Seth, who happened to pull it off the shelf of a Palo Alto bookstore. The two events were unrelated. It seems impossible that Vladimir Nabokov would have bothered to care about yet another English *Onegin*, with his own mortality very much in the balance.

In 1982, from the false azure of a clear sky came that distinctive rumble from the Montreux Palace Hotel. Forty-eight-year-old Dmitri Nabokov, Vladimir's only child and himself a decent translator, happened upon an interview with Johnston in the Moscow journal *Inostrannaya Literatura* (*Foreign Literature*). Writing from Switzerland, an outraged Dmitri unburdened himself in a breathless letter to *The Times Literary Supplement:* He quoted Johnston saying of his father's *Onegin* that "I believe he got bored doing this, so that *what set out to be a literal version in fact contains a strong element of Nabokovian* fantasy [emphasis in the original]."

Dmitri: "Johnston, in essence, accuses Nabokov of dishonesty."
Here we go again.

"It would seem imperative that Johnston, once having made
such an accusation, produce a few examples of the 'Nabokovian
fantasy' he mentions," Dmitri wrote. "I challenge him to do so."

Paul Fussell once wrote an essay called "The Author's Big Mistake." I keep a copy in my desk. Fussell collected writers' letters
of outrage sent to newspapers and magazines that had published
unfavorable—meaning, *not favorable enough*—reviews of their
work. The first sentence hardly ever deviated: "I never write letters complaining about reviews. But in this one, extraordinary
case . . ."

Dmitri simply cannot resist: "It was not my intention here to
discuss Johnston's translation . . ." We know what is coming next.
"However, I cannot forego to point out that . . ." From "among
innumerable examples," Dmitri highlights one malapropism: In
canto 7, stanza 32, his father had a team of horses "to the master coach are harnessed." Johnston rendered this, "Horses and
coaches are spliced in marriage."

"Those poor horses," Dmitri wrote. "Poor Pushkin."[1]

Sir Charles had plenty of time on his hands. His distinguished
diplomatic career, which never included an assignment to Russia,
had ended years earlier when he left the governor-generalship of
Australia. (It's possible that he practiced Russian with his beautiful
wife, Princess Natalie Bagration, the great-great-granddaughter
of Czar Nicholas I.) Johnston's rejoinder graced the *TLS* letters
page just two weeks later:

Ever since publishing my own translation of *Eugene Onegin* five years ago, I have emphasized my debt to Vladimir
Nabokov. I have a great respect for him, both as a Russian

scholar and (except in his translation of *Onegin*) as a writer in English.

But because Dmitri challenged me to come up with some examples of "Nabokovian fantasy," Johnston went on, I will be happy to oblige him.

Here are a number of words, which seem to me fantastic in the sense . . . that their quirkishness unnecessarily distracts the reader's attention away from Pushkin, and makes him think about Nabokov and his strange choice of language: *precognizing; devourment; dulcitude* and *juventude; dolent.*

Which brought Johnston to the "shotman." In canto 3 Nabokov needed to translate *strelok,* a "shooter" or "marksman." He chose "shotman."

"I looked the word up, in as heavy as possible an edition of the OED," Johnston reported:

Finally, I learned that, among other things, a shotman is one who fires the explosive charge in a Cornish tin mine. I have met Cornish tin miners in Australia, and other parts of the world, but this seems a bit far-flung. . . . What, I ask myself, what the devil is this Cornishman doing here, crouching in the bushes in the middle of the Government of Pskov? If that isn't fantasy, I don't know what is.

Dmitri—excitable Dmitri, the flashy race-car driver, the peripatetic opera singer; loyal, filial Dmitri*—roars back: "Sir Charles

---

* Who of course had plenty to say about Edmund Wilson. "I liked him," Dmitri told the visiting Martin Amis for an *Observer* interview in 1981. "He was very good with has obviously trundled his heaviest artillery into an obscure Cornish tin mine in search of an easy laugh."

In the murk of his mine, Sir Charles has stumbled upon a perfect example of Nabokovian literality: a word was needed and found that was at once technically accurate, poetically evocative, and suggestive of the proper nuance in Pushkin's *strelok*.

Cue the tiresome battle of the dictionaries. If only the world would toss out the *OED*! Webster's first definition of "shotman" is "shooter." Who would have thought?

Honoring the danse macabre choreography of the literary duel, Sir Charles then announced that he was quitting the field: "I have too much regard for the memory of Mr. Nabokov *père* to relish being provoked into a slanging match with Mr. Nabokov *fils*."

Before his figurative departure, Johnston offered an example of a "Nabokovian fantasy" that "can kill stone dead the finest effects of the original." Just as the Bollingen subeditor warned Nabokov back in 1962, his infelicity at the very end of *Onegin*, in the poet's beautiful and oft-quoted farewell to the reader (8.49), had returned to haunt him: "Whoever you be my reader—/Friend or foe, I wish with you/to part at present as a pal."

Sir Charles's unfinal word on this subject: "The English language is trickier than it looks."

That same year Berkeley's Simon Karlinsky took a potshot at "Johnson" in a *New York Times* book review, calling his *Onegin* "undeservedly overpraised by critics." Karlinsky said the 1977 translation produced "on a person closely familiar with the origi-

---

children. He was cuddly, playful. He could make a mouse out of a handkerchief and make it move for me. . . . Then his immense presumption—that he knew Russian!"

nal the effect of a Chopin nocturne played in the tempo of a military march."

I didn't translate the poem for people "closely familiar with the original," Johnston shot back. He noted that Karlinsky's view "is shared by Dimitri Nabokov, with whom, in *The Times Literary Supplement*, I am at this moment conducting a high-spirited correspondence about his father's version of 'Eugene Onegin.' "[2]

"Incidentally," Johnston added, "I was interested by Professor Karlinsky's choice of language: 'Undeservedly overpraised.' This is a fascinating bit of English usage. Can someone be deservedly overpraised? Perhaps in California?"

The *Times* had seen this movie before, and declined to publish Dmitri's riposte, which included nine side-by-side examples of how his father's *Onegin* obviously trounced Johnston's. Dmitri read the entire letter in an address to the Cornell Nabokov Festival in April 1983. It ended with the phrase, "To conclude the whole business once for all . . ."

Acknowledgments

This book sprang from a chance comment over lunch at the Café St. Petersburg in Newton, Massachusetts. Michael Johnson, a former Moscow correspondent and editor who has become a widely published Pushkin scholar, told me the story of the Nabokov-Wilson feud. As mentioned earlier, I broke out laughing.

Andrea Pitzer, a founder of the Nieman Foundation's Storyboard website and author of *The Secret History of Vladimir Nabokov*, introduced me to many of the denizens of Nabokovland. She guided me through the thickets of memoirs and archives with patience and intelligence. I am very grateful.

Stephanie Sandler, Harvard's Ernest Monrad Professor of Slavic Languages and Literature, allowed me to participate in her semester-long seminar devoted to *Eugene Onegin*, a relatively rare opportunity to read Pushkin's masterpiece in Russian, with other Russian speakers. She was a superb teacher, and helped me with many questions that cropped up while I was working on my manuscript. Her colleagues James Russell, the late Daniel Aaron, and Gregory Nagy also made important contributions to this book. Boston University's Christopher Ricks recalled his 1965 review of Nabokov's *Onegin* as if it were yesterday, and enriched my understanding of the poem.

Brian Boyd, Distinguished Professor of English at the University of Auckland, New Zealand, is the undisputed dean of Nabokov studies, and a respected academician in other fields. He answered my often naive queries with indulgence and courtesy. He shared his interview notes with key actors in the Nabokov-Wilson drama who are no longer living, such as Mary McCarthy and Harry and Elena Levin. They enriched this book, and I thank him.

The Nabokov scholars Gennady Barabtarlo at the University of Missouri and Susan Elizabeth Sweeney at Holy Cross College also generously shared their work and insights with me.

Edmund Wilson's two children, Reuel and Helen Miranda, helped me when they could, and I am grateful to them. His lifelong friend Jason Epstein found time to speak with me, and clarified many details of the Wilson-Nabokov imbroglio.

Several writers shared their thoughts and resources with me, including Robert Roper, Stacy Schiff, Stephen Nichols, Ron Rosenbaum, Sarah Funke Butler, and Sasha Chavchavadze, whose grandparents witnessed the Wilson-Nabokov fireworks. My friends Joseph Kahn, Arthur Bowen, Roger Lowenstein, Julie Michaels, Ben Birnbaum, and Ronald Koltnow also provided help and advice. Thanks also to Guggenheim Foundation vice president André Bernard, to Tatiana Ponomareva at the Nabokov Museum in St. Petersburg, and to Mike Grinley, art director extraordinaire.

Vladimir Nabokov's papers reside in two archives, at the Berg Collection of the New York Public Library and at the Library of Congress. Nabokov's executor, Andrew Wylie, granted me free range of the Berg, where Joshua McKeon and Lyndsi Barnes answered my specific queries.

Library of Congress staffers Lewis Wyman, Eric Frazier, Alice Birney, Jennifer Gavin, and Margaret Kiechefer piloted me through their considerable Nabokov holdings and the Library's extensive Bollingen Foundation archive.

Edmund Wilson's papers are at Yale University's Beinecke Library; Ingrid Lennon-Pressey, Mary Ellen Budney, Karen Spicher, and Laurie Klein were my talented case handlers there. I was also helped by Jay Satterfield, Special Collections Librarian, and Barbara Krieger, both at Dartmouth College; Dean Smith at the University of California's Bancroft Library; Abhinaya Rangarajan at the University of Tulsa's Department of Special Collections; Eisha Leigh Neely and Heather Furnas at Cornell University's Carl A. Kroch Library; and Jenna Weathers and Karen Fischer at the Newton Free Library in my hometown.

I couldn't have happened upon a more talented and engaged editor than Gerald Howard, who signed on to this project and immediately proposed an outing to Edmund's Wilson's Wellfleet, Massachusetts, gravesite. (See page 11.) I have met many writers who wish they had the privilege of working with Gerry, and I am worthy of their envy. Gerry's two assistants, Jeremy Medina and Josh Zajdman, came to know me perhaps better than they might have liked, and I extend major-league gratitude to senior publicist Helen Tobin for helping us promote the book. Random House–Pantheon mobilized a small and efficient army to bring this book into print: managing editor Altie Karper, copy editor Sue Llewellyn, text designer Cassandra Pappas, production manager Romeo Enriquez, and jacket designer Kelly Blair. Thank you all very much.

Four sensational readers caught many of my early mistakes and helped smooth out some very rough drafts: Mark Feeney, Katherine Powers, David Roberts, and my wife, Kirsten Lundberg, who has learned more about Edmund Wilson and Vladimir Nabokov than she ever dreamed of knowing. What a lucky woman!

Notes

INTRODUCTION

1. Mary McCarthy interview, Dec. 1985, courtesy Brian Boyd.
2. Simon Karlinsky, ed., *Dear Bunny, Dear Volodya: The Nabokov-Wilson Letters, 1940–1971* (Berkeley: University of California Press, 2001), p. 236.
3. Jeffrey Meyers, *Edmund Wilson: A Biography* (Boston: Houghton Mifflin, 1968), p. 441.

1 THE BEGINNING

1. Robert Roper, *Nabokov in America: The Road to* Lolita (New York: Bloomsbury, 2015), p. 25.
2. Brian Boyd, *Vladimir Nabokov: The American Years* (London: Vintage, 1991), p. 18.
3. Vincent Giroud, *Nicolas Nabokov: A Life in Freedom and Music* (New York: Oxford University Press, 2015), p. 149.
4. Boyd, *American Years*, p. 20.
5. Edmund Wilson, *The Twenties*, ed. Leon Edel (New York: Farrar, Straus and Giroux, 1975), p. xxiii.
6. Ibid., p. xxv.
7. Meyers, *Edmund Wilson*, p. 319.
8. Wilson, *Twenties*, p. 157.
9. Norman Podhoretz, *Doings and Undoings: The Fifties and After in American Writing* (New York: Noonday Press, 1964), p. 36.
10. Edmund Wilson, *The American Jitters* (New York: Charles Scrib-

ner's Sons, 1932; reprint, Freeport, NY: Books for Libraries Press, 1968), p. 307.

11. Edmund Wilson, *Red, Black, Blond and Olive* (New York: Oxford University Press, 1956), p. 263.

12. Ibid., p. 219.

13. Ibid., p. 376.

14. Edmund Wilson, *Letters on Literature and Politics: 1912–1972*, ed. Elena Wilson (New York: Farrar, Straus and Giroux, 1977), p. 737 (hereafter cited as *LLP*).

15. Wilson, *Twenties*, p. 316.

16. Ibid., p. 318.

17. Rosalind Baker Wilson, *Near the Magician: A Memoir of My Father, Edmund Wilson* (New York: Grove Weidenfeld, 1989), p. 32.

18. Lewis Dabney, *Edmund Wilson: A Life in Literature* (New York: Farrar, Straus and Giroux, 2005), p. 26.

19. Ibid, p. 309.

20. *LLP*, p. xxi.

21. Ibid., p. 45.

22. Ibid., p. 82.

23. Roper, *Nabokov in America*, p. 23; Brian Boyd, *Vladimir Nabokov: The Russian Years* (Princeton, NJ: Princeton University Press, 1990), p. 121.

24. Brian Boyd, "Nabokov as Translator," http://www.usp.br /rus/images/edicoes/Rus_n01/04_BOYD_Brian_-_Nabokov_as _Translator_-_Passion_and_Precision.pdf., p. 7.

25. Vladimir Nabokov, trans., *Commentary to Eugene Onegin*, part 2, *Eugene Onegin: A Novel in Verse* (Washington, DC: Bollingen Foundation, 1964), p 130.

26. Roper, *Nabokov in America*, p 14.

27. Edmund Wilson, *The Fifties, from Notebooks and Diaries of the Period*, ed. Leon Edel (New York: Farrar, Straus and Giroux, 1986), p. 427.

28. Boyd, *Russian Years*, p. 506.

2 SUCH GOOD FRIENDS

1. Boyd, *American Years*, p. 13.

2. Karlinsky, *Dear Bunny*, p. 69.

3. Nabokov correspondence, Aug. 2, 1944, Berg Collection, New York Public Library.

4. Boyd, *American Years*, p. 571.

5. Edmund Wilson, "The Pickerel Pond," *Night Thoughts* (New York: Farrar, Straus and Co., 1961), p. 240.

6. Karlinsky, *Dear Bunny*, p. 348.

7. Ibid., p. 164.

8. *LLP*, p. 535.

9. Rosalind Wilson, *Magician*, p. 32.

10. Wilson, *Twenties*, p. 494.

11. Brendan Gill, *Here at* The New Yorker (New York: Random House, 1975), p. 254.

12. Karlinsky, *Dear Bunny*, p. 99.

13. *LLP*, p. 378.

14. Edmund Wilson, "Notes on Russian Literature," *Atlantic Monthly*, Nov. 1943.

15. Wilson letter to Nabokov, Dec. 12, 1940, Wilson Collection, Beinecke Rare Book & Manuscript Library, Yale University.

16. Karlinsky, *Dear Bunny*, p. 76.

17. Wilson letter to Nabokov, Nov. 23, 1960, Berg Collection.

18. Susan Elizabeth Sweeney, "Sinistral Details: Nabokov, Wilson, and *Hamlet* in *Bend Sinister*," Nabokov Studies 1, no. 1 (1994): 179–194.

19. Karlinsky, *Dear Bunny*, p. 232.

20. Ibid., p. 290.

21. Elena Levin interview, Oct. 22, 1990, courtesy of Brian Boyd.

22. Karlinsky, *Dear Bunny*, p. 306.

23. *The New Yorker*, Sept. 9, 1944.

24. Karlinsky, *Dear Bunny*, p. 282.

25. *New York Times*, Feb. 18, 1951.

26. Andrew Field, *Nabokov: His Life in Part* (New York: Viking Press, 1977), p. 254.

27. Karlinsky, *Dear Bunny*, p. 210.

28. Ibid.

29. Edmund Wilson, *The Fruits of the MLA* (New York: New York Review Books, 1968), p. 7.

30. Karlinsky, *Dear Bunny*, pp. 67–68.

31. Ibid., p. 208.

32. Ibid., p. 171.

33. *LLP*, p. 409.

34. Vladimir Nabokov and Alfred Appel, *The Annotated Lolita* (New York: McGraw-Hill, 1970), p. xlviii.

35. Edmund Wilson, *Upstate: Records and Recollections of Northern New York* (New York: Farrar, Straus and Giroux, 1971), p. 176.

36. Boyd, *American Years*, p. 313.

3 SEX DOESN'T SELL . . . OR DOES IT?

1. Edmund Wilson, *The Forties* (New York: Farrar, Straus and Giroux, 1983), p. 109.

2. Meyers, *Edmund Wilson*, p. 311.

3. *LLP*, p. 437.

4. Karlinsky, *Dear Bunny*, p. 189.

5. *LLP*, p. 438.

6. Gennady Barabtarlo, "Nabokov in the Wilson Archive," fn. 3, at http://revel.unice.fr/cycnos/index.html?id=1285.

7. *LLP*, p. 444.

8. Meyers, *Edmund Wilson*, p. 316.

9. Karlinsky, *Dear Bunny*, p. 215.

10. Ibid., pp. 313–314.

11. Ibid., p. 229.

12. Ibid.

13. Ibid., pp. 313, 317.

14. Harry Levin interview, Oct. 22, 1990, courtesy of Brian Boyd.

15. Karlinsky, *Dear Bunny*, p. 320.

16. Boyd, *American Years*, p. 377.

17. Karlinsky, *Dear Bunny*, p. 363.

4 WHOSE MOTHER IS RUSSIA ANYWAY?

1. Boyd, *American Years*, p. 371.

2. Roper, *Nabokov in America*, p. 246.

3. Boyd, *American Years*, p. 648.

4. Ibid., p. 613.

5. "Legend and Symbol in 'Doctor Zhivago,' " *Encounter*, June 1959.

6. Stacy Schiff, *Véra (Mrs. Vladimir Nabokov)* (New York: Modern Library, 2000), p. 244.

7. Ibid., p. 243.

8. Ibid., p. 244.

9. Boyd, *American Years*, p. 386.

10. Karlinsky, *Dear Bunny*, pp. 222, 223.

11. Edmund Wilson, *The Triple Thinkers* (New York: Noonday Press, Farrar, Straus and Giroux, 1976), p. 200.

12. Karlinsky, *Dear Bunny*, p. 23.

13. *LLP*, p. 535.

14. Edmund Wilson, *The Cold War and the Income Tax: A Protest* (New York: Farrar, Straus and Company, 1963), p. 115.

15. Edmund Wilson, *The Sixties* (New York: Farrar, Straus and Giroux, 1993), p. 295.

16. Boyd, *American Years*, p. 480.

17. *Newsweek*, June 25, 1962.

5 MEET *EUGENE ONEGIN*

1. Eugenia Ginzburg, *Journey into the Whirlwind* (New York: Harcourt, 1967), p. 295.

2. Andrei Sinyavsky, *Strolls with Pushkin*, trans. Catharine Theimer Nepomnyashchy and Slava Yastremski (New Haven: Yale University Press: 1993), p. 92.

3. Nabokov, *Onegin* "Commentary," part 1, p. 137.

4. Nabokov, *Onegin*, vol. 1, p. 7.

5. Quoted in James Russell, "Iranians, Armenians, Prince Igor, and the Lightness of Pushkin," *Iran and the Caucasus* 18 (2014), p. 364.

6. Karlinsky, *Dear Bunny*, p. 139.

7. Ibid., p. 253.

8. *The New Yorker*, Jan. 8, 1955.

9. Boyd, *American Years*, p. 23.

10. Karlinsky, *Dear Bunny*, p. 355.

6 WHAT HATH NABOKOV WROUGHT?

1. *New York Times*, June 20, 1982.

2. Brockway letter, Oct. 1957, Bollingen Archive.

3. Brockway letter, Feb. 1958, ibid.

4. Wormer letter, July 29, 1963, ibid.

5. Schiff, *Véra*, p. 214.

6. Douglas Hofstadter, *Le Ton Beau de Marot* (New York: Basic Books, 1997), p. 268.

7. Nabokov, *Onegin* "Commentary," pp. 229, 462.

7 "HE IS A VERY OLD FRIEND OF MINE"

1. All three letters are in the Nabokov correspondence, Berg Collection.

2. Vladimir Nabokov, *Strong Opinions* (New York: McGraw-Hill, 1973), p. 240

3. Letter from Lise to "Dear Anne," Aug. 8, 1962, Nabokov correspondence, Library of Congress.

4. Letter from William McGuire to Vladimir Nabokov, May 22, 1963, Berg Collection.

5. Vladimir Nabokov, *Vladimir Nabokov: Selected Letters, 1940–1977*, ed. Dmitri Nabokov and Matthew Bruccoli (New York: Harcourt Brace Jovanovich, 1989), p. 345.

6. Ibid., p. 358.

7. *LLP*, p. 277.

8. Karlinsky, *Dear Bunny*, p. 245.

9. Ibid., p. 284.

10. Ibid., p. 290.

11. Edmund Wilson, "Pushkin," *A Window on Russia* (New York: Farrar, Straus and Giroux, 1972), pp. 15–27.

12. Stanley Edgar Hyman, *The Armed Vision* (New York: Alfred A. Knopf, 1948), quoted in Karlinsky, *Dear Bunny*, p. 233.

13. Ibid., p. 652.

14. Karlinsky, *Dear Bunny*, p. 17.

15. Walter Arndt, trans., *Eugene Onegin* (Woodstock, NY: Ardis Publishers, 2002) , p. xv.

8 WE ARE ALL PUSHKINISTS NOW

1. Vladimir Nabokov, "A Reply to My Critics," *Encounter*, Feb. 1966.

2. Edmund Wilson, *New Statesman*, Jan. 5, 1968.

3. Nabokov, *Selected Letters*, p. 424.

4. Nicholas Dawidoff, *The Fly Swatter: How My Grandfather Made His Way in the World* (New York: Pantheon, 2002), p. 201.

5. Ibid, p. 201.
6. Boyd, *American Years*, p. 215.

9 UNTIL DEATH DO US PART

1. Nabokov, *Selected Letters*, p. 393.
2. Sweeney, "Sinistral Details," pp. 179–194.
3. Dabney, *Edmund Wilson*, p. 471.
4. Meyers, *Edmund Wilson*, p. 461.
5. Wilson, *Sixties*, p. 718.
6. Ibid.
7. Wilson, *Income Tax*, p. 92.
8. Alfred Kazin, *New York Jew* (New York: Alfred A. Knopf, 1978), p. 238.
9. Boyd, *American Years*, p. 381.
10. Ibid., p. 365.
11. Roper, *Nabokov in America*, p. 246.
12. Richard Hauer Costa, *Edmund Wilson: Our Neighbor from Talcottville* (Syracuse, NY: Syracuse University Press, 1980), p. 149.
13. Schiff, *Véra*, p. 308.
14. *LLP*, p. 733.
15. Martha Duffy interview for *Time*, undated, Berg Collection.
16. Nabokov's list of "suggested" changes to Field's draft is in the Berg Collection.
17. Karlinsky, *Dear Bunny*, p. 254.

10 JUST KIDDING?

1. Wilson, *Income Tax*, p. 12.
2. Schiff, *Véra*, p. 183.
3. Boyd, *American Years*, p. 46.
4. Nabokov, *Speak, Memory* (New York: Everyman's Library, Alfred A. Knopf, 1999), p. 248.
5. Boyd, *Russian Years*, p. 509.
6. *New Statesman*, Dec. 1967.
7. "Nabokov in the Wilson Archive," at http://revel.unice.fr/cycnos/index.html?id=1285.
8. *New York Times*, Jan. 16, 1972.

9. *New York Times*, Feb. 6, 1972.
10. Ibid., Mar. 5, 1972.

11 WHY?

1. Field, *Life in Part*, p. 25.
2. Roper, *Nabokov in America*, p. 256.
3. *New York Times*, July 5, 1977.
4. Nabokov, *Selected Letters*, p. 374.
5. Boyd, *American Years*, p. 495.
6. George Steiner, "[article title?], *The New Yorker*, Dec. 10, 1990.
7. Vladimir Nabokov, *The Eye* (New York: Vintage, 1990), preface.
8. Paul Theroux, *Sir Vidia's Shadow: A Friendship Across Five Continents* (Boston: Houghton Mifflin, 1998), p. 39.
9. Elena Levin interview, Mar. 22, 1983, courtesy of Brian Boyd.
10. Undated Martha Duffy dispatch for *Time* cover story, May 23, 1969, Berg Collection.
11. Boyd, *American Years*, p. 48.
12. Letter from Edmund Wilson to F. Scott Fitzgerald, Oct. 21, 1933, *LLP*, p. 231.
13. *LLP*, p. 478.
14. Ibid., p. 497.
15. Ibid., p. 309.
16. Ibid., p. 653.
17. Theroux, *Sir Vidia's Shadow*, p. 99.

12 AS I WAS SAYING . . .

1. *Times Literary Supplement*, Sept. 3, Sept. 17, Oct. 1, Oct. 15, 1982.
2. *New York Times*, Nov. 14, 1982.

Index

188 Index

ABOUT THE AUTHOR

ALEX BEAM is a columnist for *The Boston Globe* and a former Moscow correspondent. He is the author of two novels about Russia, *Fellow Travelers* and *The Americans Are Coming!*, as well as three works of nonfiction: *American Crucifixion; Gracefully Insane;* and *A Great Idea at the Time,* the latter two both *New York Times* Notable Books. He has also written for the *International Herald Tribune, The Atlantic, Slate,* and *Forbes/FYI.* He lives in Newton, Massachusetts, with his wife and three sons.

A NOTE ON THE TYPE

The text of this book was set in a typeface called Aldus, designed by the celebrated typographer Hermann Zapf in 1952–1953. Based on the classical proportion of the popular Palatino type family, Aldus was originally adapted for Linotype composition as a slightly lighter version that would read better in smaller sizes.

Composed by North Market Street Graphics,
Lancaster, Pennsylvania

Printed and bound by RR Donnelley,
Harrisonburg, Virginia

Designed by Cassandra J. Pappas